$500

A CENTURY OF
LIONEL
TIMELESS TOY TRAINS

Dan Ponzol

Photography by Bill Milne

a Friedman Fairfax/Ziccardi book

a Friedman Fairfax/Ziccardi book

Friedman/Fairfax Publishers
15 West 26th Street
New York, New York 10010
212/685-6610   Fax: 212/685-1307
www.metrobooks.com

Library of Congress Cataloging-in-Publication available upon request.

ISBN 1-56799-966-2

Editor: Nathaniel Marunas
Creative Director: Jeff Batzli
Design Director: Kevin Ullrich
Designer: Lori Thorn
Photography Director: Chris Bain
Photographer: Bill Milne
Production Manager: Richela Fabian Morgan

Color separations by Fine Arts Repro House Co., Ltd.
Printed in Hong Kong by Midas Printing Co., Ltd.

10 9 8 7 6 5 4 3

Distributed by Sterling Publishing Co., Inc.
387 Park Avenue South
New York, NY 10016-8810
Orders and customer service 800/367-9692
Fax: 800/542-7567
E-mail: *custservice@sterlingpub.com*
Website: *www.sterlingpublishing.com*

above: The automatic gateman is one of the most popular, not to mention one of the longest-lived, Lionel accessories of all time. Its first incarnation, the all-metal No. 45, was produced from 1935 to 1942, and then after World War II from 1945 to 1949; it was subsequently redesigned and offered again from 1950 to 1966 in plastic as No. 145. The latter design was reissued in 1987 and 1988 and then again in 1994 as No. 12713. This latest version, which continues to be produced today, does the same thing—and does it every bit as reliably—as its predecessors: when a train rolls by, the gateman opens the door to his shack, steps out, and waves his illuminated lantern.

page 2: The No. 1862 027 gauge model (1959–1962) of the famous Civil War locomotive the *General* trundles through a tunnel, its colorful cow-catcher ready at the fore. This legend of American railroading was also offered over the same period in a Super O version, the No. 1872, which featured superior detailing and Magne-Traction. A third, uncataloged variation, the No. 1882, was also offered in 1960 and was identical to the No. 1862 except in its color scheme.

page 7: This street scene from Lionel's Visitor Center layout is a tribute to the legendary Madison Hardware store, the most famous retailer of Lionel trains and accessories.

DEDICATIONS & ACKNOWLEDGMENTS

I would like to dedicate this book to my father, Dante Ponzol, who in 1955 gave me the best Christmas present I would ever get: an electric train set.

I would also like to acknowledge the contributions of the following people: Larry Wotring, the last of the old time Lionel repair men, who taught me everything I know about fixing Lionel trains at the now-defunct Pollard's Firestone Tire Company in Allentown, Pennsylvania, which had a Lionel department for fifty years; Shawn Solderitch, with whom I had many conversations about A.C. Gilbert's American Flyer during which we shared and expanded our knowledge of American Flyer trains; and Alan Campbell, with whom I bought many Lionel trains over the years, increasing our knowledge about the many varieties and variations that exist. I am also grateful to Lionel's Todd Wagner, who kindly vetted these pages for accuracy, and Chuck Horan, who lent invaluable assistance during the photo shoot at the Lionel collection in Detroit.

Special thanks are also due to the many people who gave us access to their collections, including Richard Kughn and the Carail Museum, Al Galli of Train Gallery Auctions, and especially Bill Winkle, who was kind enough to allow us to see and to photograph his incredible array of postwar Lionel locomotives, trains, and accessories. Best of all, Bill let us shoot them on his breathtaking layout, which words cannot describe.

Finally, I want to thank my wife, Kimberly, for her patience during the writing of this book, and my boys—Alex, Alastair, and Daniel—for all the much-needed help they gave me with my computer.

—Dan Ponzol

I'd like to dedicate this book to several people: first, to my father, Tony "the Milkman" Ziccardi, who surprised my brother, Donald, and me with our first two sets of Lionel trains on Christmas Day, 1953; second, to my mother, Anna, for allowing her three boys to set up a 4' X 8' layout in our three-room railroad apartment in Brooklyn; third, to my partners, Jim Maione and Al Diamond, who encouraged me to undertake this project and supported my efforts to make it a reality; and finally, to my wife, Marie, and my three children—Anthony, Annmarie, and Nicholas—for their support and love.

—John Ziccardi

CONTENTS

THE MAGIC OF LIONEL TOY TRAINS

There are few childhood toys that have proven to be more enduring than the electric train. From the very beginning of railroading, the train has been a near-universal childhood plaything—the toy train seemed to appear in toy stores around the world within moments after the first fire-belching contraption gave the horse and coach a run for its money. Made of wood or tin, these primitive trains were little more than newfangled pull toys, but what they represented was something far more important: the faith of mankind in its ability to overcome physical obstacles through new industrial technology.

The steam locomotive was born of the industrial revolution, a period of promise for a better tomorrow through heavy industry. The United States expanded from sea to shining sea along the ribbons of steel laid down by the railroads, while in other parts of the world similarly sweeping changes were wrought. As art imitates life, so the toymakers imitated the technological realities of the day and took advantage of the fascination that society had with this transportation machine—a device that at once changed the lives of people around the world. Toy trains, it seemed, were destined to become an indispensable part of childhood.

The toy version evolved along with the real train, and floor toys were soon replaced by clockwork trains that circled the living rooms of America on their very own tracks. The biggest step in the evolution of the toy train came when it was adapted to run on electricity, the world's newest power source. Before long, there arose a large host of toy train manufacturers fighting for their share of the market for this marvelous new toy. From the beginning, European firms, particularly German companies, sought to export their trains into the United States, which by 1900 already boasted of a large number of firms competing in the marketplace.

No European firm, however, ever succeeded in dominating the U.S. market. Prior to World War I, the German firms—Marklin and Bing, among others—had great success selling their products in the United States. That ended abruptly, however, when the United States entered World War I on the Allied side and trade with Germany ceased. Seizing the opportunity, the American Toy Manufacturers Association convinced President Woodrow Wilson's administration not to ban toy manufacturing during the war, and domestic manufacturers quickly moved to fill the gap created by the exit of the Germans. This assured that American producers would dominate the domestic market from then on. The German companies never regained the position they had held before World War I.

As the American market matured, one manufacturer moved to the forefront and became a dominant force in the American toy train industry, ultimately outlasting all of its original rivals and evolving into an American legend. That company is Lionel.

AN AMERICAN CLASSIC

This book is a celebration of the 100th anniversary of Lionel Toy Electric Trains. Few companies in the field of playthings have had as dramatic an impact upon American culture. The story of Lionel is a story about the development of the United States from the Age of Progress onward. The uniqueness of Lionel is unparalleled in the history of the American toy industry. While certain toys have made impressions on the period of American history in which they emerged, and some have even enjoyed a nostalgic longevity, no corporate name has come to be as clearly identified with a whole range of toys as has the name Lionel.

above: The No. 154 highway flasher has probably graced more Lionel layouts than any other accessory. Low priced and attention-getting, the item flashes to signal the approach of a train at a grading crossing. The No. 12888 grade crossing signal is the current version of the popular accessory, which has been in continuous production since it was introduced.

right: The cutting-edge technology, bold looks, and bright graphics that characterized the Lionel trains of the 1990s are all in evidence on this Soo Line SD-60M loco from 1997.

duced by Lionel are illustrated—the images presented here are meant to convey an impression of the range of items produced during specific eras, not to provide comprehensive documentation. Beyond trains, other Lionel products are also pictured to help readers better understand the sales philosophy of Lionel. Competing toymakers have been mentioned only in regard to their interaction with or influence upon Lionel. There has been no attempt made to detail the histories of these rivals except where they and Lionel have crossed paths in the economic arena.

So sit back, relax, and "return with us to those thrilling days of yesteryear," when toy trains signaled the arrival of the holidays and when the most expensive toy any child usually could hope to own was a Lionel electric train set. When a father gladly spent a month's wages on a train set for the "boy," fully intending to play engineer himself as soon as the boy got the box open and the track laid. When every department store had a Toyland, and near Santa's chair a train circled about a toy village and hundreds of little children peered over the rope barricade or pressed their noses to the store window to watch it run.

Mere mention of the name usually elicits a comment like, "Lionel—oh, toy trains." The story of Lionel is also a story about the ideals and values that have made the United States of America great. It is a tale of the benefits reaped from hard work and diligence. It is a testimonial to perseverance and the rewards to be found in pursuing a dream. It is an American success story.

The information used in compiling this text was drawn from a variety of sources. Unfortunately, the sources were not always in agreement, and in some cases, specific aspects of the history were not dealt with fully or were omitted

entirely. Since this work is a celebrtion of the company's centennial, it was not conceived as the definitive work on the history of Lionel trains, but rather as an overview of the company's development and the way its products reflect the eras in which they were produced.

Items photographed for this book span the decades. Because this is not a price guide, the rare and the common have been given equal weight—they all played a role in making Lionel great, some because of design or engineering innovations, some simply because they enabled Lionel to maintain a healthy sales lead over its rivals. Similarly, not all the toys pro-

above, left: This unusual pocket edition of Lionel's 1928 catalog is just the right size for slipping into the vest pocket when shopping for a holiday train.

above, right: Produced from 1950 to 1968, the No. 310 billboard set featured miniature signs advertising real products from the time period, including Lionel's own.

opposite: Made in 1994, the No. 18119 was a reissue of the famous fiftieth anniversary Alco Union Pacific AA diesel set, which copied the original in every detail, including the die-cast frame. The Union Pacific yellow and gray color motif has long been a favorite of model railroaders.

CHAPTER ONE

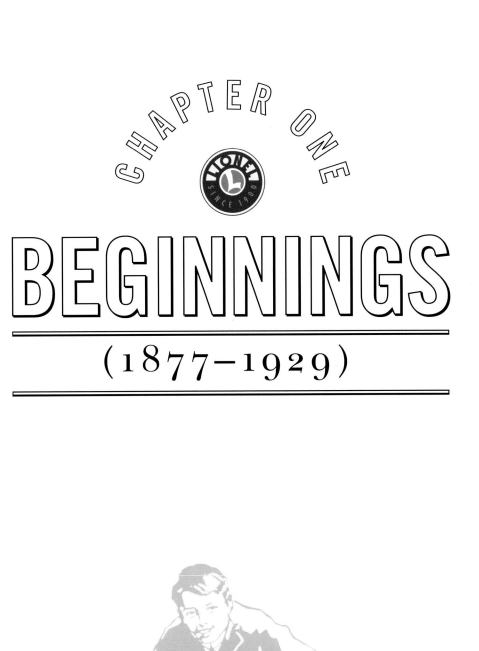

BEGINNINGS

(1877–1929)

The founder of the Lionel Corporation, Joshua Lionel Cohen, was born on New York City's Lower East Side on August 25, 1877, the eighth of nine children. As a youth, Cohen—who changed his name to Cowen later in life—fell under the spell of the age in which he lived. At this time, technology was moving ahead by leaps and bounds, and it was generally believed that this progress was benefiting mankind and could provide great rewards for the inventor and tinker. Cowen was particularly fascinated with electricity and the workings of the steam engine.

According to an oft-told story, a youthful experiment in building a working model steam engine resulted in an explosion that nearly destroyed Mrs. Cowen's kitchen. Not one to be distracted by setbacks, young Joshua continued to pursue his interest in tinkering and invention by attending Cooper Union, a New York school that focused on science and the arts. Here Cowen boasted that he invented what may have been the first practical electric doorbell for the home, only to be told by his instructor that such an invention did not have any practical value and would not be of interest to the American home owner. Cowen dropped the idea. This turned out to be only one of several profitable ideas that Cowen would turn away from while searching for the invention that would make him financially secure.

Cowen entered the engineering program at Columbia University after finishing three years at Cooper Union. The studies at Columbia, however, apparently failed to hold young Cowen's interest—he quit the engineering school and went to work for the Acme Electric Light Company, one of the premier electrical appliance producers in America and a pioneer in applying the newly developed source of electrical power to various household and commercial applications. He was hired as an assembler, but he made time on the side to work on inventions of his own design.

The turn of the century was a heady time; technology and science were changing the way man looked at the world. Industrial progress was seen as the answer to the ills of human society. Electricity was the latest manifestation of this progressive spirit. It seemed to have unlimited potential to help improve human society.

The great fascination society had with electricity explains why Cowen was so interested in

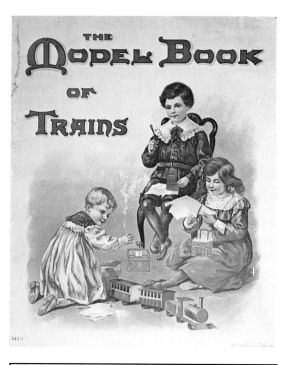

page 13: **The lead unit of the magnificent No. 18119 Union Pacific AA set (1994) pulls into view.**

pages 14–15: **This valuable No. 150 0-4-0 locomotive was based on the New York Central's long-lived S-2 Class electric loco. The series of Lionel models based on this NYC workhorse lasted roughly twenty-seven years, beginning in 1910.**

above: **In its earliest days, Lionel advertised its products in generic catalogs like this one, usually issued by an electrical supply wholesaler. These catalogs—very hard to find today—are the earliest official record of what the company produced.**

opposite: **This is the No. 100 electric loco model known as B&O No. 5 (1903–1905). Twelve inches long with maroon paint and gold lettering, it was patterned after an 1800-horsepower prototype used by the B&O and was among the first locomotives Lionel sold commercially. Needless to say, it is very scarce today, since so few survived the ravages of time and little hands.**

its applications. The whole field seemed to hold the promise of financial rewards for the inventor bold enough and clever enough to find new and profitable applications. Cowen's first commercial success came when he was eighteen, when he developed a fuse to ignite photographers' magnesium powder, which was used to provide the lighting needed to take a picture. This was before flash bulbs existed; the photographer would stand under a cloth covering while holding aloft a tray of flash powder. When ignited, this powder was supposed to burn up in a quick flash of brilliant light. The first problem was igniting the powder in a reliable and consistent manner each time. The second was the danger involved: magnesium was not a very safe substance to light by under any conditions. Cowen's fuse igniter provided safe and reliable ignition of the flash powder. Somehow, the U.S. Navy got wind of this invention and summoned Cowen to Washington, D.C. It seemed that the military was seeking a reliable mine fuse, and the young inventor's photo fuse fit the bill. Cowen was awarded a contract to produce 24,000 fuses for naval mines.

Cowen quit his job at Acme, opened his own shop at 24 Murray Street in downtown Manhattan, and soon filled the order. This resulted in working capital and a fully equipped shop, but he had nothing to do until the next order for fuses arrived. He resumed tinkering with electricity while searching for a marketable product. The next idea he developed was a battery-powered plant illuminator—a metal tube with a light bulb in one end that could be concealed in a flowerpot and used to provide accent lighting for the plant. Restaurateur Conrad Hubert, an early customer, became so interested in the product's potential that he sold his restaurants so that he could devote himself to selling the device. The product attracted some sales at first, but Cowen eventually lost interest and according to one account (there were several) sold all rights to the design to Hubert. After he obtained ownership of the patents, Hubert found a better use for the

device: he redesigned the plant illuminator as a flashlight and started the Eveready Company, which soon become a major manufacturer of flashlights. Cowen had turned away from another million-dollar invention.

After selling the illuminator patents, Cowen continued trying to find a product that he felt would guarantee him success in the marketplace. He concentrated on electric fans, and soon perfected a miniature motor to use in his fan design. The fan failed. As Cowen himself put it, "It was the only draftless fan ever made.

You could sit right in front of it and feel no breeze whatsoever." However, the design of the fan's motor was flawless, and Cowen began considering other possible uses. Since he had been interested in railways since his youth, his mind turned to using the motor to power a miniature toy train.

In 1900 he developed his first toy train item, a small wooden gondola car with a motor concealed beneath the floor. The body was built by the well-known toy company Converse. The powered gondola car, called the Electric Express,

was offered along with a thirty-foot (10m) circle of 2⅞-inch (7.3cm) gauge brass track (called Striptrack) as an attention-getting display for store windows.

Because his electric train required a complicated setup, Cowen did not envision it as a child's toy. He sold the first set to a small novelty shop for six dollars. It worked very well as an attention-getter, and orders soon started coming in. The original customer ordered more and a large order—twenty-five sets—was placed by a Rhode Island firm. This showed Cowen

that his idea was indeed marketable, that there was great interest and excellent sales potential. Realizing that this was the niche he had been seeking, Cowen turned all his attention to creating working, model railways. The Lionel Manufacturing Company was formed, and thus began the life of one of the great trademarks of American industry.

When Lionel began manufacturing toy trains, there were already several firms engaged in the same activity. Carlisle & Finch had been making toy trains in Ohio since at least 1896. The Ives Company of Bridgeport, Connecticut, had been in the toy business, and had been producing trains as floor toys since the 1880s. In 1905 the number of competitors increased when the Baltimore firm Voltamp began production of electrically powered toy trains.

As word spread of the new electrically powered Lionel train car, Cowen's reputation grew. Many of these early Lionel trains were sold as window displays, but others were purchased as toys. With the large increase in orders, Cowen had to add workers and increase his modest factory space. The demand was so great, in fact, that Cowen was soon taking orders for train items before they were even produced. In 1900 or 1901 Cowen issued his first catalog. The 1902 catalog featured the trains and some accessories, including the famous 340 suspension bridge and City Hall Park trolley.

In 1903 the first Lionel animated car (that is, a car that did something other than just go around the track), the Mechanical Derrick Car, appeared. In 1904 Cowen hired Mario Caruso as manufacturing supervisor, marking the beginning of a long and productive relationship. By 1905 Lionel's sales reached $8,000 per year, a good return for a startup company with a product new to the American market. To advertise, Cowen capitalized on his original idea for the train—he began setting up larger displays of his products in store windows. Orders soon came pouring into the factory.

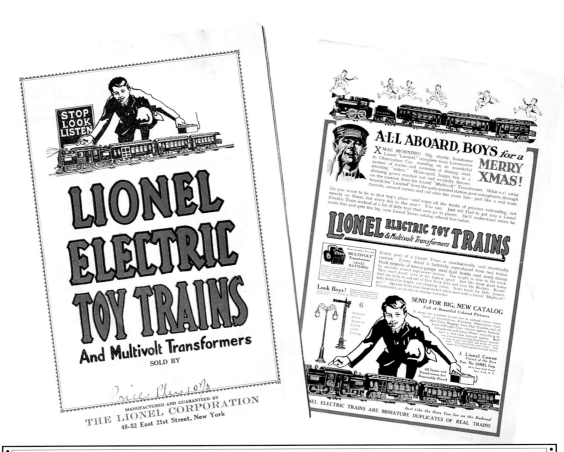

opposite: The No. 1 trolley is another piece from the early days of Lionel (1908–1910). It must be remembered that streetcars were the most common form of public transportation at this time, so it is no wonder that Lionel chose to reproduce them in miniature. This car is a four-wheel, six-window version with open platforms, a streetcar design common to most larger American cities. Lionel sold large numbers of these early trolleys and they helped build the company's reputation. The cars should not be dismissed due to their crude appearance—considering the look of the average toy in 1908, Lionel trolleys were on the cutting edge of toy design.

above: Lionel advertising evolved into a recognizable pattern as the company progressed through the 1920s. Shown here is a promotional piece featuring the "Lionel Boy" logo (left), for which Cowen's son was the model. Also shown is the famous "Lionel Conductor" (right, circa 1917–1920), calling to all boys to jump aboard a Lionel train for a happy holiday season.

The public liked the trains, but it soon became clear that batteries were not a satisfactory power source given the short life they had in the early 1900s. Cowen began looking for a way to use household electricity to simply and safely run the trains. The problem was that no simple transformer existed that would do the job, so Cowen had to invent one. The first Lionel transformers ran too hot, but later models were modified so as to be safe for home use. The perfection of the transformer was an important innovation in model railroading; it made battery-powered trains a thing of the past.

The combination of transformer and train had been made possible in 1906, when Lionel decided to replace two-rail track with three-rail track. This simplified the electric train manufacturing process and allowed for more efficient pickup of electrical power from the rails. Cowen called the three-rail track "Standard Gauge" and had the name patented. Largely due to Lionel's clout, this new design was soon copied by other manufacturers and was partly responsible for the future success of model railroading. It also inspired a great advertising slogan for Lionel: "Standard of the World."

In the first several years of production, most Lionel trains did not follow any particular real-life design. In 1907, however, Lionel brought out what is considered the first model of a real train—a toy version of the locomotive that was in use on the Baltimore & Ohio's Camden line. This early quest for realism would become a hallmark of Lionel trains that has continued up to the present day. Cowen moved the plant to nearby 4 White Street to gain badly needed additional manufacturing space, and power

machinery was added for the shaping and stamping of metal parts and bodies. Also in 1907, Cowen's son Lawrence was born. Larry would later become the "Lionel Boy" featured on most prewar Lionel packaging.

In 1908 Lionel expanded its product line to include a cattle car, a boxcar, a Pullman car, a flatcar, and a gondola car.

In 1910 growth once again forced to Lionel to seek larger quarters. This time the factory was moved to New Haven, Connecticut, while the offices remained in New York City. Also in 1910, Lionel began to offer electric locomotives based loosely upon the design of the New York Central type-S electric engine. This is viewed as a momentous decision for Lionel because for the next twenty years they would issue locomotives based upon this prototype, each more realistic than the last.

In 1912 Lionel made two important moves. First, Cowen issued the company's first multi-color catalog. Second, in an attempt to diversify his offerings, Cowen produced one of the first racing model automobiles using a form of slotted track. While this was an attention-getter, it did not win huge sales for the company and it was eventually dropped from the offerings. It seemed that the American public firmly identified Lionel as a toy train company.

In 1913 the American public spent $300,000 on Lionel trains and accessories. The following year, growth forced another move, this time to Newark, New Jersey; in a cost-

cutting move, the offices and factory were recombined.

The Ives Company, a competitor to Lionel, had introduced O gauge trains, which were half the size of the standard gauge items, in 1910. The size of standard gauge had always limited its sales. The reduction in size meant that the same layouts—featuring track, trains, and accessories—could be built in a smaller space. Cowen was quick to realize that smaller trains pointed the way to the future, and in 1915 he introduced a line of O gauge Lionel trains to compete with the Ives models. By entering the O gauge market, Lionel was now in direct competition with several other smaller train manufacturers, such as American Flyer and Hafner. Train sales continued to soar. In 1917 the firm moved into a new factory building in Hillside, New Jersey; its staff at the time numbered some 700 people. Its toys were now known across the nation and were the best-selling trains on the market.

In 1916 the trade group Toy Manufacturers of America was founded, and A.C. Gilbert of Erector set fame became its first president. The association was instrumental in convincing the U.S. government to allow producers to continue making toys once the country became embroiled in World War I. But that didn't mean that making toys was all these manufacturers did. The goverment contracted Lionel to produce various items for the war effort, including periscopes, compasses, navigation instruments, and material for the Signal Corps.

Interestingly, even though a tie-in would have been natural, Lionel refused to become deeply involved in manufacturing war toys. Cowen disliked military toys and did not favor producing them as a regular product line, but his marketing people convinced him to produce a military train because of the war effort. Lionel's armored locomotive and cars met with mixed sales and were discontinued soon after the war ended; Lionel did not make war toys again until the late 1950s.

above: **Multivolt transformers were one of the keys to Lionel's success in selling many train sets in the early years of the company. Toy transformers at this time (including some of Lionel's early efforts) were usually unreliable, and quite often dangerous, devices. The Multivolt transformer featured high-quality materials and a safe, simplified design for the first time in children's electric toys.**

opposite top: **With its ads in the early 1920s, Lionel was among the first toy companies to directly target the ultimate consumers of its toys: young boys. Here a youth wearing knickers swells with pride as he races to share his new Lionel train set with his neighborhood friends. This kind of direct appeal to youngsters would be characteristic of Lionel's advertising throughout the company's history.**

opposite bottom: **This is a modern reissue of the No. 7 brass and nickel loco (1910–1923) from the early days of Lionel, when some locos were offered in brass finishes. Original brass locos are not easy to locate, as most people opted for the more realistic black finish. The No. 7 represented Lionel's commitment even in the early period to using high-grade materials and the survival of these locos is a testament to their quality.**

As a result of Lionel's contracts with the government, the company grew so large that reorganization was required. In 1918, it became the Lionel Corporation, with Cowen as president.

The 1920s were boom years for the United States. The citizenry wanted to put the horrors of the First World War behind them. America seemed to be holding a huge, unending party characterized by reckless living and self-gratification. Whether this was true of the train-buying public or not, one thing was certain: Americans were in the mood to buy consumer goods in record numbers, and toys were no exception.

In the time leading up to the stock market crash in late 1929, business in the United States was thriving. Overall sales climbed and output increased. Among the major toy companies, competition for the loyalty of toy buyers became intense. To attract buyers required ingenuity and skill. In 1921 Cowen hired a sales manager, Arthur Raphael, who became responsible for getting Lionel trains into millions of homes across the nation.

An interesting aspect of the early expansion of Lionel is the code names that were assigned every item in the catalog. This was done so that when orders were telegraphed across the country, model numbers would not be read incorrectly. This system would remain in operation for several years.

In 1923, as part of continuing efforts to improve production and lower costs, Lionel established La Precisa in Italy to provide high-quality tooling and stamping as well as die-casting models. La Precisa later became responsible

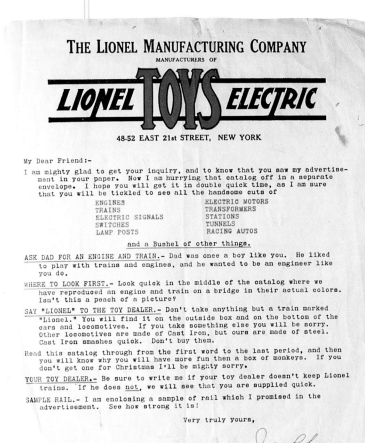

THE LIONEL MANUFACTURING COMPANY

MANUFACTURERS OF

LIONEL TOYS ELECTRIC

48-52 EAST 21st STREET, NEW YORK

My Dear Friend:—

I am mighty glad to get your inquiry, and to know that you saw my advertisement in your paper. Now I am hurrying that catalog off in a separate envelope. I hope you will get it in double quick time, as I am sure that you will be tickled to see all the handsome cuts of

ENGINES	ELECTRIC MOTORS
TRAINS	TRANSFORMERS
ELECTRIC SIGNALS	STATIONS
SWITCHES	TUNNELS
LAMP POSTS	RACING AUTOS

and a Bushel of other things.

ASK DAD FOR AN ENGINE AND TRAIN.— Dad was once a boy like you. He liked to play with trains and engines, and he wanted to be an engineer like you do.

WHERE TO LOOK FIRST.— Look quick in the middle of the catalog where we have reproduced an engine and train on a bridge in their actual colors. Isn't this a peach of a picture?

SAY "LIONEL" TO THE TOY DEALER.— Don't take anything but a train marked "LIONEL." You will find it on the outside box and on the bottom of the cars and locomotives. If you take something else you will be sorry. Other locomotives are made of Cast Iron, but ours are made of steel. Cast Iron smashes quick. Don't buy them.

Read this catalog through from the first word to the last period, and then you will know why you will have more fun then a box of monkeys. If you don't get one for Christmas I'll be mighty sorry.

YOUR TOY DEALER.— Be sure to write me if your toy dealer doesn't keep Lionel trains. If he does not, we will see that you are supplied quick.

SAMPLE RAIL.— I am enclosing a sample of rail which I promised in the advertisement. See how strong it is!

Very truly yours,

Joshua L. Cowen

President.
THE LIONEL MFG. CO.

---

for moving Lionel out of the pressed-steel age and into the die-cast period of its history.

Also in 1923, Lionel redesigned its trains, powering them with a better motor. While the original Cowen design had been in use from the company's inception, the trains were now expected to pull more cars and to operate under play conditions. A new motor, hyped by Lionel as a "Super Motor," was designed and became the core of the new Lionel line. Also, the new locomotives were designed to incorporate more structural support in the form of cross bracing inside the loco body, giving the products greater strength and durability.

In 1924, always seeking out new talent, Lionel hired Frank Pettit as a designer. Pettit would go on to develop the famous postwar Vibrotor motor system, and to become chief

of Lionel's development team until retiring in 1959.

In 1925 Lionel celebrated twenty-five years of train sales. That same year, a new threat to Lionel's position arose when a new company, Dorfan, began manufacturing trains. Dorfan's products were unique in the toy train world—they were made of high-pressure zinc alloy die-castings (a move copied by the other toy companies) and designed so they could be taken apart and reassembled. Lionel met this challenge head-on by issuing its own "Bild-a-Loco," which allowed young train owners to build their own locomotives from factory parts.

Unfortunately for Dorfan, several factors worked against the company's becoming a real threat to Lionel. First, their offerings were limited. Second, the die-casting alloys suffered greatly from the rigors of play and disassembly. Finally, Lionel had a presence and financial power far beyond that of the new company. These factors would doom Dorfan to a short moment of fame in the history of toy trains.

In 1927 Lionel opened its famous factory showroom at 15 East Twenty-Sixth Street in New York City. Here all the newest Lionel products could be displayed to the public and to prospective toy buyers. Having a permanent showroom for toy trains was a unique concept, and it showed the confidence that Lionel had in its product line. The strength of sales seemed to support Lionel's decision to take this plunge into public relations.

The growth in popularity of Lionel trains was in no small part due to the creative use Cowen made of advertising to convey the message of a quality product at a fair price. Lionel's most serious competitor at this time was the Ives Company, which produced a very successful line of trains and toys. Cowen rightly recognized Ives as his company's main challenger. Starting in 1915, Lionel catalogs began to compare the quality of Lionel's trains to that of other such products. In this ad campaign, Lionel criticized its competitors' products as insufficiently robust

for the vigor of little hands and touted its own—made of heavy-gauge sheet metal—as being able to take all the abuse that a child could dish out. If released today, these ads would probably violate the truth in advertising law, but this was the nature of ad campaigning in the early 1900s. There is little doubt that the ads were directed primarily at Ives. Exactly how successful these ads were is not clear, but we do know that Ives'

SILVER JUBILEE
1900–1925

THIS year marks the Twenty-fifth Anniversary of The Lionel Corporation.

We extend our sincerest thanks to our patrons who have contributed so largely to our success, and who make us proud of our achievement in perfecting the line of Model Electric Trains and Railroad Accessories recognized as "Standard of the World."

This, our Silver Jubilee Year, will be made memorable by our new line, pre-eminently the finest ever produced, representing the culmination of experience gained through concentrated effort on one specialized product for a quarter of a century.

Literature and descriptive matter of the marvelous new 1925 line will be ready for mailing in the near future. Samples are on display at our permanent Toy Fair, occupying the entire sixth floor at 48-50-52 East 21st Street, New York City.

STANDARD OF THE WORLD SINCE 1900

LIONEL ELECTRIC TRAINS
MODEL RAILROAD ACCESSORIES
"MULTIVOLT" TRANSFORMERS

PRICES ALWAYS LOWEST CONSISTENT WITH QUALITY

above left: The advertising approaches taken by Lionel were unique for their day. This letter, written by Cowen himself, was mailed out to thousands of boys who had answered an advertisement offering a free sample of Lionel track in order to demonstrate its superiority to the competing brands.

above: Lionel took every opportunity to put its trademark names in front of the American public, as with this commemorative broad sheet from the silver jubilee in 1925.

opposite: The armored loco and cars (1917–1921) were the only foray into military-type trains Lionel undertook until the late 1950s. The armored loco was designed to cash in on the patriotic fervor generated by World War I and was based loosely on a real type of armored train. It sold well enough, but Cowen didn't like war toys, and he turned away from such offerings for almost thirty years.

LIONEL

Beginnings

sales in the toy world were in decline during this period. The classic anti-Ives Lionel ad showed an Ives cast loco ending up in many pieces on the floor after diving off the tracks, while the Lionel took the same fall and remained in great shape.

Cowen also seemed to be aware of the importance of a company's image—in addition to criticizing other companies' products, the Lionel ads showed an idealized view of the Lionel factory as a gigantic enterprise, stretching for what seemed like blocks. These ads conveyed a sense of power and strength that few other train companies could match. Perhaps surprisingly, none of Lionel's competitors responded to the ads; this gave Lionel even greater credibility in the eyes of the American consumer. Finally, Lionel became the first toy company to use full-color ads in the comics sections of Sunday newspapers, reaching out to the younger audience directly.

The Lionel-Ives conflict was resolved in 1928, when Ives declared bankruptcy. The firm's position in the toy train market had been declining for some time, due in no small part to the inroads Lionel was making. Ives' profit margin was also suffering because of the company's labor-intensive manufacturing techniques: its toy boat hulls, for instance, were soldered together instead of being formed on a metal press in one piece, and extensive die-casting was used on its loco frames, which added to the production cost. Also, Ives remained committed to the production of high-quality clockwork, or windup, trains; even though the firm was under intense competition from many sources that were able to offer a cheaper product, Ives refused to lower the quality of its mechanical clockwork lines. The losses suffered in this field impacted on the electrical lines as well.

New capital and partners were desperately sought to help improve Ives' financial position, the company was reorganized, and the Ives family's control was decreased. Nevertheless, Ives still found itself in a downward spiral. The climactic event came in 1928, when the Blanchard Printing Company of New York sued Ives for nonpayment of the 1926 catalog printing. The result of the suit was bankruptcy for Ives; the company's collapse also caused its competitors to take action.

The demise of this rival should have been cause for rejoicing, but Cowen and the other toy makers of the day knew that Ives could easily be reborn and returned to its former glory if a competent, well-financed group stepped in to take over the Ives plant. To prevent this from happening, Lionel and American Flyer, the other major toy company of the day, joined together to purchase Ives at the bankruptcy sale. It was an odd union, but they knew that a revitalized Ives did not serve the interests of either company. Ives was in debt for $200,000 and had an outdated plant and production style, but keeping it from falling into the hands of another rival group was essential.

Much has been said about the partnership Lionel and American Flyer formed to carve up the remains of Ives. It has been suggested that

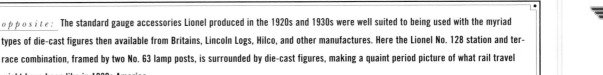

opposite: The standard gauge accessories Lionel produced in the 1920s and 1930s were well suited to being used with the myriad types of die-cast figures then available from Britains, Lincoln Logs, Hilco, and other manufactures. Here the Lionel No. 128 station and terrace combination, framed by two No. 63 lamp posts, is surrounded by die-cast figures, making a quaint period picture of what rail travel might have been like in 1920s America.

above: The 1924 catalog cover showed a race between the No. 402 electric and the family dog. While the size of the train in relation to the boys and the dog is slightly exaggerated, Standard Gauge trains were pretty big—a lot of room was needed to construct the large layout depicted.

Interestingly, it seems that A.C. Gilbert got involved behind the scenes due to his interest in the distribution rights for Meccano, a Lionel-owned English building set that competed for sales with Gilbert's Erector set line. According to various reports, the auction proceedings were held up while Lionel's representative had more money sent in the form a timely cashier's check from Gilbert's Connecticut bank. (Then later that year, Gilbert acquired the Meccano Company from Lionel, ending any threat to his Erector set line.)

The Ives assets were purchased for $73,000. The group of New England businessmen cried foul because of the irregular nature of Lionel's funding, but the bid was upheld. Lionel and Flyer ran the Ives factory to fulfill orders from that year's toy show; the factory, however, proved not to be up to the task, and Lionel and Flyer had to mix and match items from their own lines to complete the Ives offerings.

The precise amount of money provided by each member of the partnership was never revealed, but the Ives patents were divided up between American Flyer and Lionel, with the reverse unit patent going to Lionel.

For Cowen, the Ives crisis worked out very well—one major challenger was now gone, and an important patent had been acquired. But the

the banks involved were influenced by Lionel and American Flyer and therefore became the principals in the division. Whether there was a secret toy cabal or not—it has been said that Hafner and Dorfan, two smaller train manufacturers, were involved in some peripheral way, but

this is largely speculation—there is evidence that both A.C. Gilbert (owner of American Flyer) and Lionel stood to profit from the deal.

Meanwhile, competition came in the form of a group of New England businessmen who wanted to keep the Ives factory in operation.

opposite top: The No. 187 bungalow set (1930s) is representative of the highly detailed tin-stamped buildings Lionel produced before World War II. A whole village in a box, the set featured such lithographic details as shingles for the roofs of the houses and vines on the walls.

right: Lionel was among the first toy companies to offer its own line of transformers for use with its electric train sets. In time Lionel transformers became legendary for their safety and efficiency. The Multivolt model featured on this catalog cover was among the first generations in this long family line.

below: The No. 402 electric locomotive was the first big twin-motored electric engine Lionel produced in their Standard Gauge era. This advertising picture shows the locomotive paired with an early series of cars.

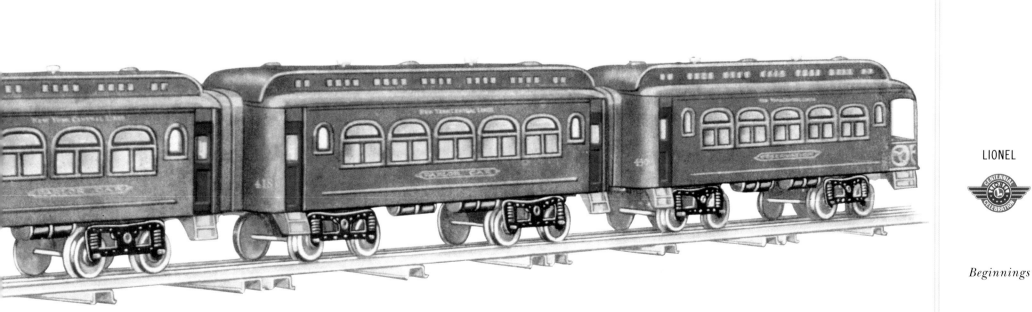

above: Introduced in 1925, the Bild-A-Loco and Bild-A-Motor kits allowed a boy to completely assemble a loco body and motor. Some locos were offered as kits for the owner to assemble; the motor could also be assembled as a stationary electrical motor if desired. This advertising postcard was issued to extol the features of these new designs to prospective buyers at the 1928 Chicago Toy Fair.

right: The 408E and State cars represent the high point of the standard gauge tinplate period, and no modern standard gauge collection is complete without them. The 408E was a brute, with two Super Motors capable of pulling the State cars with ease. The State cars themselves (so called because they were named after four states) were the largest tinplate standard gauge passenger cars Lionel ever made. Slightly longer than the Blue Comet cars, they featured full interiors. This 408E has a reverse unit, as signified by the "E," which meant electric reverse.

field was not entirely clear. True, the number of serious competitors was rapidly shrinking. Carlisle & Finch had left the train market in 1915, while Voltamp sold its train line to Boucher, which adopted Lionel's Standard Gauge track (calling it Wide Gauge) and offered the revised train line as a deluxe product aimed at the high-end consumer. American Flyer, however, loomed large on the horizon.

Located on Halsted Street in Chicago and owned by W.O. Coleman, the American Flyer Manufacturing Association was ready to compete directly with Lionel in both O and standard gauge trains. Until the demise of Ives, American Flyer had held a distant third-place position, but after the collapse of the Connecticut firm and

the subsequent financial fray, it moved into the number two spot determined to undermine Lionel's market share. Even though Lionel got the most new sales as a result of Ives' bankruptcy, American Flyer did not make a poor showing. Many consumers liked its products. The central location in Chicago eliminated the bottlenecks Ives had faced in getting its products out of New England to market. And like Lionel, American Flyer advertised in magazines and papers. Indeed, American Flyer would prove to be much tougher than Ives had been, and on the eve of the Great Depression Lionel found itself battling its rival for market shares.

In fact, up until 1966, American Flyer would be Lionel's greatest competitor, challenging

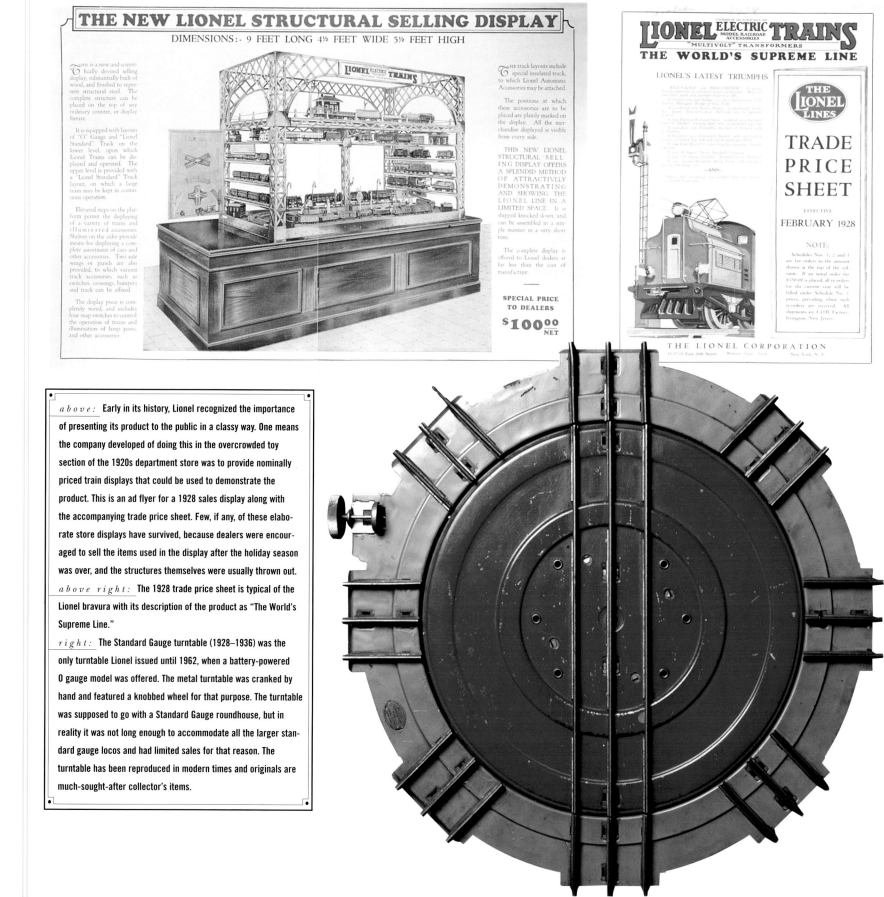

THE NEW LIONEL STRUCTURAL SELLING DISPLAY

DIMENSIONS: 9 FEET LONG 4½ FEET WIDE 5½ FEET HIGH

This is a new and scientifically devised selling display, substantially built of wood, and finished to represent structural steel. The complete structure can be placed on the top of any ordinary counter, or display fixture.

It is equipped with layouts of "O" Gauge and "Lionel Standard" Track on the lower level, upon which Lionel Trains can be displayed and operated. The upper level is provided with a "Lionel Standard" Track layout, on which a large train may be kept in continuous operation.

Elevated steps on the platform permit the displaying of a variety of trains and illuminated accessories. Shelves on the sides provide means for displaying a complete assortment of cars and other accessories. Two side wings or panels are also provided, to which various track accessories, such as switches, crossings, bumpers and track can be affixed.

The display piece is completely wired, and includes four snap switches to control the operation of trains and illumination of lamp posts, and other accessories.

The track layouts include special insulated track, to which Lionel Automatic Accessories may be attached.

The positions at which these accessories are to be placed are plainly marked on the display. All the merchandise displayed is visible from every side.

THIS NEW LIONEL STRUCTURAL SELLING DISPLAY OFFERS A SPLENDID METHOD OF ATTRACTIVELY DEMONSTRATING AND SHOWING THE LIONEL LINE IN A LIMITED SPACE. It is shipped knocked down, and can be assembled in a simple manner in a very short time.

The complete display is offered to Lionel dealers at far less than the cost of manufacture.

SPECIAL PRICE TO DEALERS

$100.00 NET

LIONEL ELECTRIC TRAINS
MODEL RAILROAD ACCESSORIES
"MULTIVOLT" TRANSFORMERS
THE WORLD'S SUPREME LINE

LIONEL'S LATEST TRIUMPHS

THE LIONEL LINES

TRADE PRICE SHEET

EFFECTIVE

FEBRUARY 1928

NOTE:

THE LIONEL CORPORATION

above: Early in its history, Lionel recognized the importance of presenting its product to the public in a classy way. One means the company developed of doing this in the overcrowded toy section of the 1920s department store was to provide nominally priced train displays that could be used to demonstrate the product. This is an ad flyer for a 1928 sales display along with the accompanying trade price sheet. Few, if any, of these elaborate store displays have survived, because dealers were encouraged to sell the items used in the display after the holiday season was over, and the structures themselves were usually thrown out.

above right: The 1928 trade price sheet is typical of the Lionel bravura with its description of the product as "The World's Supreme Line."

right: The Standard Gauge turntable (1928–1936) was the only turntable Lionel issued until 1962, when a battery-powered O gauge model was offered. The metal turntable was cranked by hand and featured a knobbed wheel for that purpose. The turntable was supposed to go with a Standard Gauge roundhouse, but in reality it was not long enough to accommodate all the larger standard gauge locos and had limited sales for that reason. The turntable has been reproduced in modern times and originals are much-sought-after collector's items.

Cowen's company at every turn and forcing healthy competition upon the American toy train market. American Flyer's claim to fame was its excellent lithographed tinplate passenger cars. While American Flyer never matched Lionel's variety of standard gauge equipment (which was called wide gauge by American Flyer, because of Cowen's patents), it stressed consumer satisfaction with the products it did offer. On their name plates, for instance, the American Flyer cars featured such slogans as "thousands of happy boys," implying widespread acceptance of their product by the youngsters of the United States.

To counter the rising threat from American Flyer, Lionel developed ever more elaborate train sets and constantly improved the detail of its equipment. Lionel also took the lead in developing accessories; Cowen believed that children would quickly tire of train sets that consisted only of a train and a circle of track. Lionel put so much emphasis on toys to go with the trains that quality accessories became an enduring hallmark of the company. Cowen was not content to imitate what others did; he wanted to innovate, to be the leader in the train hobby field. He saw Lionel setting a standard in model trains that others would have to follow.

As the end of the decade neared, Lionel appeared to be strong. However, the Jazz Age was almost over, and there were signs that the financial health of the nation was not what it should be. The collapse of the Florida land boom had been the first great economic calamity since the end of the war. While it did not ruin a huge number of Americans, it still cast a dark shadow over an otherwise continued ten years of economic growth. The situation in Europe also held warnings for any who cared to take notice. The harsh reparation terms imposed on Germany by the Treaty of Versailles had helped ruin that nation's economic health and was having repercussions across the Continent. The fas-

cist government of Mussolini had risen to power in Italy, and even its rigid organization of the state could not ensure economic well-being. Most Americans blithely ignored the clouds on the distant horizon. The party went on, the spending continued, hardly anyone thinking that one day it might all come to a shocking and dramatic end.

The collapse of the stock market in 1929 heralded the start of the Great Depression. While the crash was only one manifestation of a series of economic ills that had been allowed to develop in the United States over the decade, it is recognized as the start of the prolonged period of economic despair that gripped the United States up to the coming of World War II.

The post–World War I boom in consumer spending had been buoyed by the overconfident "live for today" attitude of the American public. The Depression ended this attitude for most Americans. The companies whose profits were based on consumer spending were now facing a difficult time. America in general could not continue to spend at pre-1929 levels, so a shifting of markets and pricing had to occur. In this new and highly unpredictable economic environment, even a minor incorrect business decision could doom a company.

It was in these murky economic waters that Lionel found itself as the 1930s dawned. All the old ways were gone; each company would have to chart a new course for itself in this new age.

Beginnings

above: The No. 516 standard gauge hopper (1928–1940) is an example of the high-quality metal stamping work Lionel used in manufacturing its train line. Note that even the individual coal pieces are depicted in the stamped-metal load.

above: Trade price sheets played an important role in retail selling before the war, when discounting was not yet a common practice and most stores sold items at list cost. For the manager of a toy department, these sheets were indispensable for planning the holiday selling season, and were usually available at that year's Toy Fair or shortly thereafter. This 1929 sheet, from the year of the stock market crash, features a classic illustration of a boy playing with a No. 408 electric loco.

right: The No. 390E is one of the medium-level Standard Gauge locomotives that were common to many sets between 1929 and 1931. While not as impressive in size as the 400E, it was still very popular during this time period. The 390 was released in several paint schemes, but a black boiler was the most common. For modern collectors, this is one of the more readily available prewar Standard Gauge pieces. However, condition is an all-important consideration. The most common defect in this model seems to be frame deterioration due to poor metal composition. A buyer must always check that the loco frame is straight and true.

CHAPTER TWO

FROM THE
DEPRESSION TO
WORLD WAR II
(1929–1942)

The Depression had the same impact on Lionel as on every other American company. No one had ever experienced so devastating and long a period of economic decline. The country saw a rapid collapse not only of prosperity but also of hope for future progress. The toy companies were worse off than most firms because their sales depended on discretionary spending, a luxury most families no longer enjoyed.

By 1930 Lionel had assumed complete control of Ives, which Cowen envisioned transforming into a lower-cost line to compete with American Flyer and, to a lesser degree, such smaller rivals as Hafner. Lionel put a large sum of money into this Ives reincarnation, but Cowen was never fully committed to competing in the low-cost market. As a result, the 1931 Winner line (inexpensive, low-quality electric trains built on Ives-tooled bodies), designed to fill just this niche, did not succeed.

The main reason Lionel had been so interested in the Ives Company was its patented reverse unit. Designing reverse units had long been a major problem for the manufacturers of AC current trains. DC current is relatively easy to reverse due to its magnetic field, but for AC—in which the relationship of the brushes had to be reversed each time you wanted to change direction—reversal was an engineering nightmare. Given the state of electronics in 1920s America, there was no easy solution. A variety of different systems came and went. Lionel had developed a bulky pendulum reverse system,

but the best system—in size and performance—was the Ives reverse, or "E-Unit," as it later came to be called.

More accurately described as a sequential relay, the Ives system worked on a gravity principle in which a coil pulled up a pawl each time the coil was electrified. This in turn engaged a drum with a star wheel on its center, which rotated insulated and uninsulated sections in contact with six copper fingers. The relationship of the fingers to the drum determined

if the motor to which they were wired would run forward or reverse, or remain in a neutral position. An engineer at Westinghouse named H.P. Sparks had developed this system. The key to the Sparks patent was a neutral position between forward and reverse. Ives had obtained rights to this system in 1924, and all other train companies were left with the daunting prospect of solving the problem by other means. Dorfan had invented a reverse unit using DC current and rectifiers to trigger the reverse sequence, but it was cumbersome. All the other reverse units, including Lionel's pendulum reverser, allowed only forward or reverse, so the loco would slam from one direction to another when activated—not exactly good for gears and motors. The prize of the Ives reverse was well worth all the effort put into the acquisition of the Ives assets—the unit serves even to this day and was the core electrical component around which the reputation of Lionel's durability was built. Lionel also received the right to the Ives name and tooling for some Standard Gauge equipment.

As a condition of the buyout Lionel was required to make some use of the trade name so that it would not revert to the public domain. Lionel met this condition with some reticence, and used the name only in obscure ways, most notably on the reverse side of the track locks used to hold tracks together—the undersides of these items were marked "Ives" until the 1970s. In 1933 Lionel shut down the Ives plant, closing the book on this famous American toy producer.

pages 34–35: This No. 390E Blue Comet (1929–1931, 1933) featured a Bild-a-Loco motor and came in several color combinations; the rarest is the two-tone green variation.

above: Lionel aimed its advertising at as diversified a market as possible, and as a result all types of magazines during the 1920s through the 1940s carried Lionel ads. So while *The Literary Digest* might seem an odd place to put a Lionel ad, it was in keeping with Lionel's advertising philosophy.

opposite: The Lionel standard gauge No. 217 caboose (1926–1940) shows the attention to detail that made Lionel the preeminent prewar train manufacturer. It displays ladders and railings in brass, marker light lens holders, and inset doors and window frames. Each of these pieces required a separate metal stamping tool, in addition to those needed to form the body, floor, and roof. In today's economy the cost of manufacturing such an exquisitely detailed item would be staggering. This pea green iteration is from 1926.

The Lionel catalogs reflected a changing attitude from 1933 onward, when Lionel became one of the first toy companies to turn to radio advertising to help sell its product. The 1933 catalog introduced buyers to Jimmy and Mike, who would take listeners on a great railway adventure twice a week. "Two times each week, Jimmy, a Lionel engineer, climbs into Mike's cab to hear the old engineer relate these exciting stories." The radio program aired on Sundays and Wednesdays from November 5 to December 20, 1933.

The 1933 catalog also reflected certain changes taking place in the Lionel train line. The sensation of the year was the "Chugger," an electrical device fitted to the premium locos that was capable of making a vaguely chugging sound. The other feature was "Distant Control," remote reversing on selected locomotives, a feature that later became standard on most toy trains.

The catalog prominently featured the blue National Recovery Act eagle, indicating that Lionel products were in keeping with the rules and regulations of President Roosevelt's recently passed act and that Lionel was helping the United States to recover from the Depression. The classic Blue Comet and State sets appeared this year in Standard Gauge.

Lionel also launched *The Lionel Magazine*, which provided tips for building model railroads. For fifty cents, a boy received a subscription along with a nifty Lionel pin and certificate. The club boasted members in "every state in the union, Canada, South America, England, Australia,

Africa, China and Japan." This magazine was replaced in 1937 with the famous *Model Builder* magazine, which remained in publication until after World War II. This magazine reflected the changing American tastes concerning model trains, especially the continuing shift toward greater realism.

The 1933 catalog was also important because it was the first to announce Lionel's entry into the field of girls' toys. "Sister can now have a Lionel Range to make her happy. Solidly constructed of steel and with a high-grade

porcelain finish. Oven walls are heavily insulated with asbestos keeping the exterior cool. It can bake, broil, and has two open burners." Lionel's entry into the field of nontrain toys reflected the cultural values and gender stereotyping of the period. Boys were expected to be involved with the technological aspects of society, while girls were guided into the role of domesticity. The stove was a high-quality toy for its time (the firm could boast about asbestos because at the time people were not aware of its carcinogenic nature). The stove vanished after a short run in the Lionel catalog.

Unfortunately, however, the Depression was not kind to any toy manufacturer, and despite its marketing efforts Lionel was eventually faced with bankruptcy. In 1934, Cowen placed the company in receivership. The story has long been circulated that Lionel was saved from collapse by the manufacture and sale of the Mickey Mouse handcar and other lower-cost trains that tied into the great popularity enjoyed by Walt Disney productions. In 1934 Lionel did indeed issue a Mickey Mouse handcar, along with a variety of other Disney-themed items, including the Mickey Mouse circus train outfit. But while there is no doubt that sales of the handcars helped Lionel through a very dark period, simple math shows that these items alone could not have saved Lionel from financial ruin. The handcar sold for about one dollar. To suggest that millions of them were sold borders on the ludicrous. Certainly, the sales of popular Mickey Mouse

opposite: The No. 300 Hellgate Bridge accessory (1928–1942) is the most awe-inspiring pressed steel toy ever made by Lionel. A copy of the real bridge located in New York City, it is highly authentic and its huge span causes it to dominate any train layout it is installed on. The reissue of the bridge (in 1999) was widened to accommodate two O gauge lines and its towers were illuminated.

above: Along with a membership certificate and a bronze member button, *The Lionel Magazine* was offered as a perk of membership in Lionel's Engineer's Club in 1932. The magazine offered "thrilling stories of true adventures of famous railroad men" as well as how-to articles and advertisements, all for the reasonable cost of fifty cents.

items went a long way toward helping turn around Lionel's sluggish sales, but it is also clear that the Disney campaign was only part of a clever reorganization plan that saved the company. (This plan was so ingenious, in fact, that it garnered praise from the bankruptcy judge after Lionel was discharged from bankruptcy.)

Other facets of the plan reflected the advent of the streamliner and extensive use of die-castings. The M10000 Union Pacific streamliner was introduced in 1934. Designed by General Motors for special light-duty service on the Union Pacific, it was in every sense a monument to modern progressive technology. From the unique articulated design to to the streamlined art deco shape, the M10000 represented modern railroad engineering's best achievements. The locomotive and cars were permanently attached through a special truck and vestibule design. This gave the train the illusion of being a continuous wormlike machine that bent around curves like a living creature. It was powered by the new diesel engine, which was slowly appearing on the railroad scene and was causing great ripples in the steam-driven locomotive world. When the M10000 was displayed at the 1934 Chicago Century of Progress, thousands of visitors marveled at its radical design.

The M10000 was used in many advertisements for a variety of products. It got wide press coverage across the nation, and was imitated in one streamlined train after another. All of the American railroads jumped on the bandwagon. The idea of streamlining had captured the interest of the American public, and soon everything from toasters to streetcars was being streamlined as a symbol of modernity. It was hardly surprising, then, that Cowen turned his attention to the original streamliner as a way of getting his company back on firm financial footing. The Flying Yankee was next, a smaller model than the M10000, and a copy of the Boston & Maine's entry into the world of articulated and stream-

above: Disney products were all the rage in 1934, when the No. 1100 Mickey Mouse handcar was introduced. It became a big seller for Lionel, and was instrumental in helping the company recover from receivership. Other similar models soon followed, such as Donald Duck, Santa, and Chickmobile handcars. These were part of the popularly priced "Lionel Jr." line, which evolved into Lionel's 027 gauge train line.

lined trains. It was followed by the Commodore Vanderbilt, a streamlined steam locomotive that vaguely resembled the NYC loco it copied. The real gem of the scale-streamlining era was Lionel's Milwaukee Road Hiawatha loco, which was done in magnificent O scale.

In order to highlight the scale aspects of these items, Lionel introduced its scale "T-rail" for the streamliners to run on. Designed to accompany the O scale 700E Hudson, the ultrarealistic T-rail was like actual track (and unlike the hollow, tubular Standard Gauge track) in that it was made of solid metal and was joined in the same way as real track. To complement the new designs, Lionel also unveiled its famous locomotive whistle, which became a hallmark of Lionel trains. Toy train manufacturers had struggled for years to get sound into their locomotives. Lionel had already released its Chugger sound maker, but no toy train had an authentic-sounding whistle. When Lionel introduced the whistle to the public in 1935, it was an instant success.

As usual, Lionel moved quickly to protect itself against imitators: the ingenious design was patented, preserving the technology for Lionel's exclusive use. Lionel engineer Charles Giaimo

above: A popular seller during the Depression, the legendary Mickey and Minnie Mouse handcar (1934–1937) helped Lionel achieve sound financial footing at a time when many toy companies were closing their doors. Even though many of the cars were sold, they are hard to find today. The figures of Mickey and Minnie were made of a fragile composition material and are often missing or broken. In addition, the cars were made to be low-priced children's toys and were played with more frequently (and perhaps more vigorously) than higher-priced electric train sets might have been.

had developed a sound chamber based on the sounds of real railroad whistles that had been recorded for study. The sound chamber produced a deep-throated railroad whistle sound when air was forced into its chambers, and was a marvel of design simplicity. A separate motor was connected to the chamber to provide for the flow of air, but the most amazing aspect of the whistle was the control feature. The entire whistle was connected to a DC relay that would not close while normal AC current was being applied to run the train. Only when a special button was pushed on the control box was DC current superimposed over the AC, causing the relay to close, the motor to run, and the whistle to blow. As long as the current to the tracks was on, the operator could blow long or short bursts whether or not the train itself was running.

The whistle was fitted into the tender, where it emitted a very appropriate sound. It was also fitted into the power cars of the streamliners, but curiously it was set up to make a steam whistle noise instead of a diesel air horn sound. Of course, in the end no one seemed to care about this slight technicality; the sound was all-important, and only Lionel had it in their trains.

Other manufacturers tried—unsuccessfully—to replicate the whistle effect in their own locomotives without violating Lionel's patent. The W.O. Coleman Company, owner of American Flyer prior to the A.C. Gilbert acquisition, attempted to develop a whistle system that relied on a multiple-railed track section to sound the whistle. This clumsy and inconvenient system required the user to install this special track wherever he wanted to sound the whistle, which would work only at that point on the layout. Then in 1949, Gilbert tried to develop a whistle in the tender like Lionel's, but with the relay set up differently. The idea, however, was basically the same, and Gilbert was forced to discontinue the system because it violated Lionel's patent.

Lionel's M10000 was unique in other ways as well. It was the first scale train produced by Lionel using extensive die-castings. Most trains up until this time had used some die-castings for trim, but the engines were built mostly from formed sheet metal. Through the early 1930s, Lionel had been keeping an eye on the improvements in metal die-casting, believing that it might present a way to cut costs while at the same time producing much more detailed locomotive bodies.

At the railway exhibits at the 1939 World's Fair, real-scale railroad equipment was displayed to the public for the first time. Train enthusiasts were excited at the prospect that model railway

FOR 37 YEARS LIONEL THE LEADER HAS BEEN BUILDING TO IT . . . .

FIRST AUTHENTIC SCALE MODEL OF THE MIGHTY HUDSON

PRICED TO SELL FOR AVERAGE MAN'S MONEY

opposite: The scale Hudson No. 700E is beyond a doubt the Holy Grail of Lionel trains. Intricately modeled and superbly detailed, it captures the power and look of the original. This model was Cowen's favorite, so he lavished care on its production. The fact that it commanded a list price of seventy-five dollars during the Great Depression gives some idea of the expense it took to produce this thoroughbred model. No Lionel collection is considered truly complete unless a 700E graces the roster. Lionel made several less-detailed locos between the 1930s and the 1960s, but none comes close to this museum-quality model. Difficult to find today, 700E's command top dollar.
above: The No. 700E Hudson was a spectacular item, and as such required special advertising when it was issued in 1937, during the depths of the Great Depression. This advertisement assured the consumer that the 700E was affordable by the "average man," since it was offered as a series of kits that when completed built up into the finished loco.

equipment did not have to look as toylike as it had since the start of the hobby. A renewed interest in scale detailing was sweeping the toy train world, and Lionel was positioning itself to take advantage of it.

Toy trains made out of formed sheet metal could not be given appropriate detailing, but die-casting allowed for exquisite detail to be added to regular toy trains with a minimal increase in price. Lionel had been seeking for some time to improve its lines. For this reason, the firm had helped to establish La Precisa, a tool-and-die making concern in Naples, Italy, where high-quality tool-and-die making was a highly developed trade.

Since 1904, Lionel's manufacturing division had been in the hands of a Sicilian immigrant, Mario Caruso, whose no-nonsense—even severe—supervision kept Lionel competitive for decades. At any rate, La Precisa was rumored to have been purchased by Caruso (though some think he just operated it)—rather than Cowen—in 1934. If this is true, one can only wonder if this had anything to do with Italy's emerging fascist government. Perhaps the idea of foreign control of a tool-and-die making concern would not have been tolerated as Italy moved further toward militant nationalism. Caruso, being Italian by birth, was the logical choice to purchase the company. This is only speculation, but the relationship continued under Mussolini's rule—the tooling for Lionel's scale Hudson, developed later in the decade, and the earlier sheet metal die work are reportedly from this Italian consortium. Some collectors have said that the Lionel Mojave color closely resembles Italian State Railway olive and that the curious rounded roof on the prewar boxcars is a copy of European-design rolling stock of the period.

Whatever the details, Lionel was successful in its struggle to stave off ruin in 1934 and 1935. Indeed, through a combination of good management and innovative marketing, Lionel emerged even stronger than before. The M10000 was a hands-down winner for Lionel, and even brought sales closer to pre-Depression levels. After Lionel management learned the advantages of using die-castings, plans were made for the company to move away from the "tinplate" type toy train into the more detailed die-cast locomotive boiler.

The Lionel catalogs from 1934 onward featured more and more die-cast locomotives as the production of tinplate trains was gradually halted, along with the standard gauge line. In 1935, Lionel was also focusing on the lower end of the train market. The introduction of the Lionel Jr. line gave rise to the first Lionel 027 trains, which became a lower-priced staple of the Lionel lines. Perhaps more importantly, Lionel soon became aware of the interest in accessories that actually did something as the train went by. The first such accessory that arrived on the scene—and one that remains in production today—was the automatic gateman. As the train came by, the gateman would guard the crossing with his lantern—a scene that was real enough for early highway travelers in the 1930s. The instant success of this piece showed that buyers wanted action accessories, and Lionel began to explore new ways to bring real-life action to their toy train layouts.

The 1936 catalog reflected even more dramatically the changing tastes of electric train fans. For the first time, there were no Standard Gauge electric locomotive–powered sets listed for sale; individual locos were pictured only as an afterthought at the bottom of the pages.

Left: The 700E was also offered as the 763E, a slightly stripped-down, less costly version. Pictured is the black edition; it also came in gray. The 763E omitted some applied detail on the body, and featured simplified side-rod action and a tinplate-type tender. Probably because it was more affordable, the 763E sold better than the full scale 700E and thus is easier to find today.

The cover, however, promised great things to come—it featured a new locomotive, the 700E, and blueprints, along with the Pennsylvania torpedo loco. This toy was not offered for sale; the picture was just a teaser. The following year, the 700E was revealed in all its glory, along with a rather oddly modified set of "Rail Chief" cars, which were really modified Hiawatha cars.

The New York Central Hudson locomotive engine had long been a favorite of Cowen, who had seen it at work in and around New York City. Wanting to create a scale model that would be second to none in appearance and operation, he designed Lionel's Hudson locomotive and tender, lettered for the New York Central. The whole item was die-cast, with the dies reportedly made in Italy and scaled to National Model Railroad Association (NMRA) wheel and flange specifications. It had a huge motor, and was geared to a realistic scale speed so it would not appear toylike by running at disproportionately high speeds around the track.

The 700E, available in several models, was a masterpiece of toy making. No other railroad item has ever achieved the legendary status reached by this one piece. It is the ultimate product to add to a Lionel collection even if the collector does not specialize in prewar Lionel. One model was designed to run on outside three-rail track, the preferred format for O scale operations in the 1920s and 1930s. The scale Hudson was even offered as a series of kits for those who could not afford its outlandish Depression-era price tag of seventy-five dollars. In this way a modeler could buy the kits as his pocketbook allowed and assemble the huge locomotive over a period of time, culminating with the painting and lettering of the finished model.

opposite: With its streamlined design, the real-life M10000 was a symbol of technological progress in 1930s America, and Lionel was smart to copy it and capitalize on its fame. The M10000 was the first loco to make use of die-casting techniques, and was one of the products that helped Lionel recover from the financial troubles it found itself in during this time period.

above: The M10000 was shown on the 1934 catalog cover next to a regular Lionel tinplate loco, a study in opposites. Lionel turned the corner with this and other products (especially the Disney- and holiday-themed items in the Lionel Jr. line) and at the end of the 1930s it was in a stronger market position than ever before.

Even by today's standards, the Hudson is impressive and extremely realistic. Unfortunately for modern collectors, many toy trains made of die-cast metal before World War II are prone to suffer from a deterioration common to zinc that has been combined with other metals. This condition has been described in many ways: the Germans call it zinc pest, while Americans call it zinc rot; there are also other, unprintable names. This interesting condition has to do with the quality of metallurgy at the time, in which metals of varying degrees of purity were mixed together to produce a die-cast product.

Trains that suffer from zinc rot experience a slow flaking of the castings, usually at the extremities at first. The trim and wheels seem to develop small fissures, and as the "disease" progresses the frame and boiler slowly expand, creating cracks and eventually total disintegration. It actually seems as if something is pushing the frames apart. Some experts suggest that the condition is caused by the oxidation of zinc, but whatever the cause, there is no cure. Once a casting starts to develop the signs of fatigue, it is a lost cause. Interestingly, this problem is not common to all die-cast toys of the period. Some

castings remain entirely unaffected, while others fall completely apart; on many locomotives only the wheels go bad, and on others the whole body succumbs.

In 1935, in yet another departure from trains, Lionel offered the new Lionel Craft boat—"the boat that actually steers itself." There had been a vague relationship between toy boat and toy train manufacture all through the early years of the 1900s. Most of the German train manufacturers, for instance, also offered a line of tin boats. In the United States, Ives had at one time offered an extensive line of watercraft for the junior navigator. Why Lionel decided to enter the toy boat market at this late

date is unclear. Perhaps, like the girl's stove a few years earlier, it was an attempt to diversify production during uncertain economic times. Regardless, the move seemed ill-timed, as toy boat sales had begun to decline in the years before World War II. With its boat, which featured a quality clockwork motor and self-steering mechanism, Lionel attempted to overcome the main drawback to toy boating—having the boat's motor wind down away from the shore. The Lionel device allowed the owner to preset the rudder so the boat would sail away from shore and then make a long turn back to its starting point. The runabout model was well designed, looked good, and sold reasonably

well. Lionel later offered a companion racing boat. Both boats were featured in the catalog for several years, but no other boat-related offering ever materialized, and the models vanished prior to the advent of World War II.

Another nontrain gamble Lionel made was the Lionel airplane, released in 1936. With this ingeniously designed toy, Lionel sought to capitalize on the other great area of 1930s transportation interest—flight. This monstrous toy featured a large metal pylon on the ground that held an electric motor that drove a flexible shaft connected to the airplane's propeller. The airplane could be made to take off, circle, loop the loop, and land—all by remote control. The

structure of the plane itself was weak; made of stiffened fabric, it was easily broken or distorted through continual use. Also, the tube sticking out of the pylon was too easily snapped off by little hands. The airplane came with two different bases made of heavy paper; these were the plane's airports. Due to its novelty the airplane sold well at first, but its size and fragility got in the way of lasting success, and it too vanished before the war. The design of the Lionel pylon drive, however, has been the basis for all airplane-type toys designed since.

These excursions into nontrain (and non-die-cast metal) items aside, the success of the Lionel die-cast streamliners and scale Hudson prompted Lionel to move exclusively into die-casting for all its locomotive bodies. At a time before the widespread use of plastic, die-cast metal offered the best cost-saving alternative to the labor-intensive hand assembly of sheet metal bodies.

In many ways, 1938 was a big year for changes at Lionel. The company was slowly converting all its locomotive production from pressed metal and tin to die-casting. The design emphasis had firmly shifted to real-life authenticity, and Lionel was going to take the lead in giving the public what it wanted. While tin items could still be found in the line, they were clearly on the way out. Lionel was already experimenting with plastics, which were still new to the scene in the late 1930s. The company had first used Bakelite plastic on its gateman, and use of this new wonder material would slowly creep into other items as well.

The biggest change for Lionel in 1938 was the introduction of its OO line, which marked a radical departure into a new size, smaller than O gauge. Originated in Europe, smaller trains—OO and HO (half 0) gauge—had been appearing in the marketplace for a while, and both seemed to offer advantages over their large brethren; certainly, their small size and scale were attractive to consumers. Enthusiasts of these smaller sizes, however, had to build their own or make use of primitive kits to accomplish their railroading goals. European OO trains could be had ready to run, but because they were almost all of European origin they were of little interest to the average American.

Of course, Lionel had been aware of the slow growth of OO for several years before they took the plunge. Toy companies have long spied on the competition to scoop new ideas. When a small competitor named Scalecraft began releasing easy-to-assemble OO kits and other items, Lionel quickly copied the cars and even used its competitor's products in putting together advertising and displays. Unwilling to deal with an unknown company, the larger New York toy stores readily bought the Lionel products, much to the chagrin of the Scalecraft owners. This didn't leave Scalecraft entirely out of the loop, though—due to a patent on the OO truck, Lionel was forced to pay Scalecraft a small royalty as long as the larger company's OO items were on the market.

The Lionel OO line was almost an exact copy of the 700E and scale cars developed in O gauge. Extensive die-casting was used to give the items a realistic appearance and hefty feel. The OO Hudson was a miniature gem, and the deluxe model was even fitted with the famous Lionel steam whistle. There were only four basic

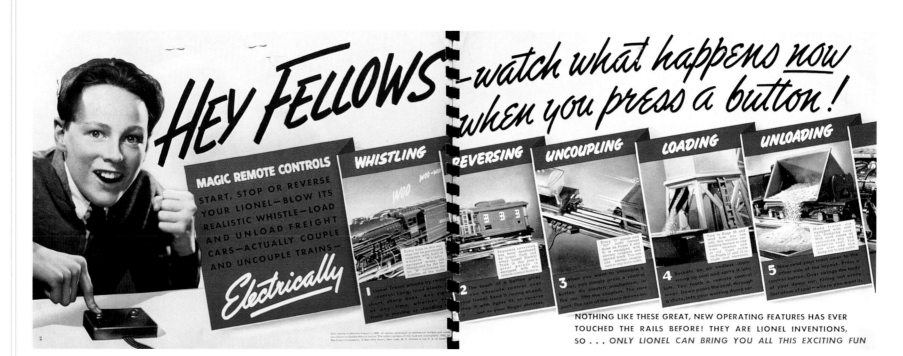

cars to choose from: a caboose, which was modeled after an American Eastern prototype; a tanker; a two-bay hopper; and a standard boxcar. No other types of rolling stock were ever developed, and this alone explains the limited success Lionel had with its OO line. The line was issued for two- and three-rail track and in scale or semiscale form—too many choices for so limited a line and one that required high-production output of the same items in four different formats. The OO Hudson was a masterpiece in its own right, but required the buyer to venture into the murky waters of the new gauge, which was not familiar to consumers and seemed not to have a variety of merchandise to offer after the train set itself was purchased. Lionel did not produce any OO accessories, although catalogs from this time suggest that the Lionel tin villas and scale crossing gates could be used with the OO trains.

When Lionel started producing its 00 line, many manufacturers were already taking a chance with HO items, though mainly in kit form. By the late 1930s, the gauge had gained a respectable following. Seeing an opportunity, A.C. Gilbert's American Flyer decided to try its hand at HO trains. It offered only one loco—a

Hudson—but several pieces of rolling stock, all in die-cast metal (and later plastic). There was a gondola, a depressed center transformer car, a reefer, a flat car with railway trucks, and New Haven passenger-type cars. Best of all, the Gilbert piece ran on any HO track. It outsold Lionel OO by a large margin, not because it looked better—Lionel was the clear winner in scale realism—but because it offered greater convenience and expandability.

When toy train manufacturing ground to a halt with America's entry into World War II, Lionel allowed the OO line to die a natural death. When the war ended, Lionel decided that the line would not be brought back and put all the OO die work in storage. Most domestic manufacturers of the gauge slowly vanished in the growing postwar sales of HO, and foreign imports fell off to nothing, forcing OO enthusiasts either to build most items from scratch or to turn to another gauge. Gilbert's HO line reemerged after the war ended, disappeared in 1950 to undergo changes, and reappeared in 1955 as a main contender for the HO market. Lionel did not take the HO plunge until 1957, too late to make an impact on the market.

In 1938, the same year that Lionel began experimenting with OO gauge, the company phased out all sheet metal bodies and Standard Gauge items, although some of these products were available from dealers for a number of years afterward.

Lionel decided on three basic O gauge types for steam locomotives. The 224 type was the smallest and offered a magnificent die-cast starter set loco; its wheels were arranged as a 2-6-2. The 225, with a feed water heater tank flared into the boiler front, was the medium-range O gauge steam locomotive; its wheel arrangement was a 2-6-2. The final member of this trio was the large 226, a heavy die-cast loco with a long die-cast tender that featured

CAR LOADING AND UNLOADING

ELECTRIC, REMOTE CONTROL COAL ELEVATOR

A SACK OF IMITATION COAL

ELECTRICALLY OPERATED REMOTE CONTROL DUMP CARS

opposite top: The 1930s saw an increase in consumer interest in remote action accessories and operation features for toy trains, as evidenced by this catalog spread from 1938. In the postwar period Lionel would focus even more on remote-controlled accessories.

opposite bottom: This 1938 catalog spread introduced Lionel OO gauge trains, an attempt to move into a smaller gauge that featured high detailing. The Lionel OO gauge items failed to catch on in the United States, however, and Lionel never brought them back to the line after World War II.

above: The No. 97 coal loader was one of the first of Lionel's popular operating accessories. Here in the 1938 catalog it is shown as a complete set along with a dumping coal car. The coal loader, with its fascinating, if frequently messy, function of loading scale coal pieces into and out of hopper cars, was carried over into the postwar line.

a realistic firebox glow imparted by a red light under the rear boiler area; its wheel arrangement was only 2-6-4.

The release of these locomotives marked the start of a new era of realism for Lionel, and these models can be considered the ancestors of the Lionel postwar loco family. While they did not smoke, they did whistle and they had automatic couplers (though of the tinplate box

style). Their real distinction, however, was their appearance—the wealth of body detail was amazing. They looked good, they ran great, and they were priced in several different ranges. The tinplate era died with the arrival of these items on the scene. Most consumers of the prewar period wanted the most realistic toy trains available, and not even the best tinplate train could hold a candle to the new

LIONEL

From the

Depression

to

World War II

die-cast kings of the rail. The changes wrought by Lionel in manufacturing techniques and in philosophy paved the way for the postwar boom in toy trains.

Realism was now the standard for toy trains, and those who did not meet it were considered old-fashioned. Lionel was in fact cutting off a vast number of tinplate toy owners from further expansion of their hobby. It is true that there was a certain amount of compatibility in the waning years of the prewar period, but after the war the break became complete. While locos could be converted to new couplers and trucks, the prewar freight cars, with some exceptions, no longer seemed worth converting, since the new offerings in the modern style were so much more attractive. The postwar toy makers blazed ahead and never looked back; there were no regrets as tinplate faded into toy train history.

When the die-cast locos arrived on the market, there arose the question of matching rolling stock. Unfortunately, the process of converting the factories was not complete when World War II brought toy making to a halt. Lionel did produce a new line of finely detailed tin cars—a tank car, an automobile boxcar, and a Pennsylvania Railroad–type caboose—to use with the new die-cast steamers. They were made of tinplate, but with their fine detailing and stamping, they represented the zenith of mass-produced pressed-steel railroad cars. Lionel also had begun to experiment with plastic as a manufacturing medium. The Madison passenger cars are an early example of plastic construction. There were also die-cast scale cars to be used with the scale series of engines. One can assume that if Lionel had not been interrupted by the war, production would have continued along these directions and

LIONEL LOCOSCOPE

INSERT FILM HERE
LOOK THROUGH LENS HERE

75 FILM VIEWS of the WORLD'S FAIR
SEEN THROUGH THE LENS of a
LIONEL LOCOSCOPE (No. 1500)

opposite: This rear view of the magnificent No. 5342 OO gauge locomotive (1938–1942) shows the care that went into Lionel's earliest foray into small-scale model trains. This detailed, three-rail version of the loco is pulling a coal tender with a whistle. Unfortunately, the onset of World War II put an end to Lionel's OO gauge efforts, which were never resumed. When Lionel finally reentered the small-scale arena in 1957 with its HO line, it was too late for the company to secure significant market share.

above: The Locoscope film viewer was an advertising premium tied into the 1939 World's Fair. The plastic loco body held a film loop which could be viewed by peering though the loco, much like the Viewmaster-type toys that still exist today. The film supplied with the loco featured seventy-five views of the World's Fair. The viewers were popular due to the great interest generated by the fair, but few survive today. Pictured is an archive sample, complete with the box in which it was issued.

the entire line would eventually have been switched over to a new scale model appearance. As it is, we can only speculate as to what might have been. Regardless, by the end of the conflict in Europe, plastics emerged as the new king of materials. From 1946 onward, Lionel was actively engaged in using this new wonder to create their new products.

Lionel's prewar changes to its product line were not, however, limited to gauge and material. A great deal of creative energy was also spent on accessories. Cowen had always been an advocate of providing young train operators with true-to-life accessories to enliven their train layouts. The early accessories, the most common of which were signal lights and buildings, did not do much except light up. After 1935 there was an explosion of intricate operating devices to use with the electric trains.

The emphasis, of course, was on real-life items that would be found around a real railroad. One of the first accessories Lionel developed was a coal loader, which copied in tin the giant coal bunkers and towers found along railroad rights of way. In the 1930s, the railroads shipped tons of coal and most people used it as a source of heat. Every American town, no matter how small, was bound to have at least one coal yard and bunker. The coal loader, designed to fit between two parallel tracks and painted in red and yellow, had a toylike look, but its operation was ingenious. After the coal car had dumped a load of coal in the receiving bin next to one track, a hidden motor drove a chain of buckets from the bin way up and into the top of the storage bunker that faced the other track. At the touch of a button, the coal could be released down the chute and into a

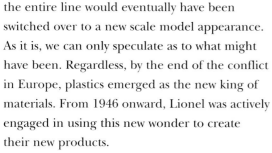

waiting car on the second track. The action—exciting and a little messy, as little pieces of artificial coal tended to be dropped around the loader from its chain buckets as they bounced their way up and into the top part of the bunker—could be repeated endlessly. To complement the bunker, Lionel released a coal-dumping car, which operated from the uncoupling-track section. A young engineer could load and unload by remote control.

The coal loader was followed by a lumber loader. Based loosely on the lumber sheds found at a sawmill or lumber company, this device, while not as realistic as the coal loader, was just as popular. It too was made to sit between two parallel tracks. On one track a dumping log car deposited logs into a receiving bin; an endless chain drive of hooks took the logs up to the holding bin; and the touch of a button released the logs into the waiting car. Like the coal loader, the log loader was painted in unrealistic colors of bright green, red, and yellow, but its operation was flawless.

Another outstanding accessory offering was the triple-action magnetic crane, a natural choice due to the large quantity of scrap metal shipped by railroads. An imposing piece, the crane towered over the rail yard and could rotate 360 degrees in either direction. Its cleverly designed mechanism, which used a motor and a solenoid clutch, allowed the operator to raise and lower the magnet, rotate the crane, and turn the magnet on and off by remote control. Like the other new accessories, the crane was painted in gaudy tinplate colors of red, yellow, and green. The crane became an operator favorite, and soon found a place in many home railways busily loading steel scrap onto gondola cars.

The last of the major new accessories built by Lionel before the war was the spectacular bascule bridge, a drawbridge that relied on a massive counterweight to help lift it into the open position whenever a ship sailed beneath it. This item was a faithful copy of real-life bascule bridges, many of which were at one time located in and

around New York City as part of the many railways leading into Manhattan from across the Jersey marshes. The bridge was fully operational, and when activated it would lift up to its full height before descending back again. For use on the floor, a channel frame (a device that guides the rails of the bridge into place after the bridge is raised and lowered) was provided so that the track could be aligned easily; the bridge was painted gray with a green base and featured a red and yellow control house with a red warning light on top.

The trend toward realism was also reflected in many other items. A new scale block signal appeared, along with a similar highway flasher. A scale girder bridge in die-cast metal was produced. A finely detailed station platform with period advertising billboards was released. The older nonscale tinplate items slowly disappeared from the catalogs, with no fanfare to mark their passing. When America entered the war, dealers still had a mixture of stock, so the tinplate items continued to be available for a short time.

When toy train production was halted in 1942, Lionel was in a position to dominate the train market in the United States. Its products were well known and were viewed as quality toys. Lionel had successfully moved out of the tinplate era into die-castings, and although that change was incomplete, the groundwork had been laid for the great postwar trains to come. The Lionel Corporation had survived the Great Depression, which had swallowed many other toy companies, and had emerged stronger than before. In addition, a successful advertising campaign, coupled with the release of its own magazine, *Model Builder*, had allowed Lionel to shape the train market by highlighting the need for scale and realism—and to demonstrate how

LIONEL

From the

Depression

to

World War II

above left: In 1942 Lionel issued a letter to the trade explaining that the catalog was smaller than usual due to the war, but that Lionel intended to keep interest in its trains alive during the war with continued promotion. The letter explained that Lionel was involved in wartime production and that train fans should look forward to the day when regular train production would resume.

above right: This is the ad folder for the Lionel paper train issued during World War II, when using steel to make toys was simply out of the question. The paper train was one of the ways in which Lionel strove to keep the public's interest in toy trains alive during the war.

opposite: This detail shows the coupling system used by the Rail Chief and M10000 cars. The articulated vestibule copied the design of the real-life train, though not the actual mechanism. As the illustration shows, each car shared a common truck. The Rail Chief cars were designed to be used with the 700E Hudson.

well its products filled these requirements.

During the war, Lionel was not content to work only on government contracts, though the firm did receive several commendations for its contribution to the war effort. Lionel also saw to it that the spirit of trains was kept alive. First, a paper train was made to help the public through the trainless war years. It was a cutout, but it was beautifully printed, designed to resemble actual items in Lionel's prewar product line, and comprised a complete set of trains and accessories. Second, throughout the war Lionel occasionally ran ads suggesting that the best was yet to come, hinting at an expanded and innovative line of trains to be unveiled after the war ended.

Interestingly, even though Lionel was seen as an innovative and responsive toy company, there was one real-life change to the railroads that the firm did not enthusiastically copy: dieselization. Before the war, the only venture taken by Lionel in the realm of dieselization involved the streamliners. Lionel made no attempt to copy road or yard diesels, even though many railroads were employing them in yard and switching duties by 1942, and some were allowing passenger and freight service behind a big "growler," as the diesels were affectionately called. Joshua Lionel Cowen was a steam man, and he apparently did not enjoy the growing popularity of diesels. It wasn't until after the end of World War II, when the widespread presence of diesels could no longer be ignored, that Lionel finally started producing models of them—and they were very successful.

above: The Lionel Railroad Planning Book was issued at the end of the war to help boys start designing their new, larger postwar layouts in anticipation of the time when Lionel would resume full train production. Building this sort of hype was instrumental to Lionel's advertising efforts during the war.

right: Lionel's prewar O gauge tinplate line reflected the Standard Gauge line in makeup and composition. Pictured here is an O gauge prewar electric No. 252. Many people bought the smaller O gauge prewar trains instead of the Standard Gauge, as they were cheaper and took up less space. O gauge would eventually replace Standard Gauge as the cornerstone of the Lionel line.

CHAPTER THREE

THE POSTWAR PERIOD

(1945–1969)

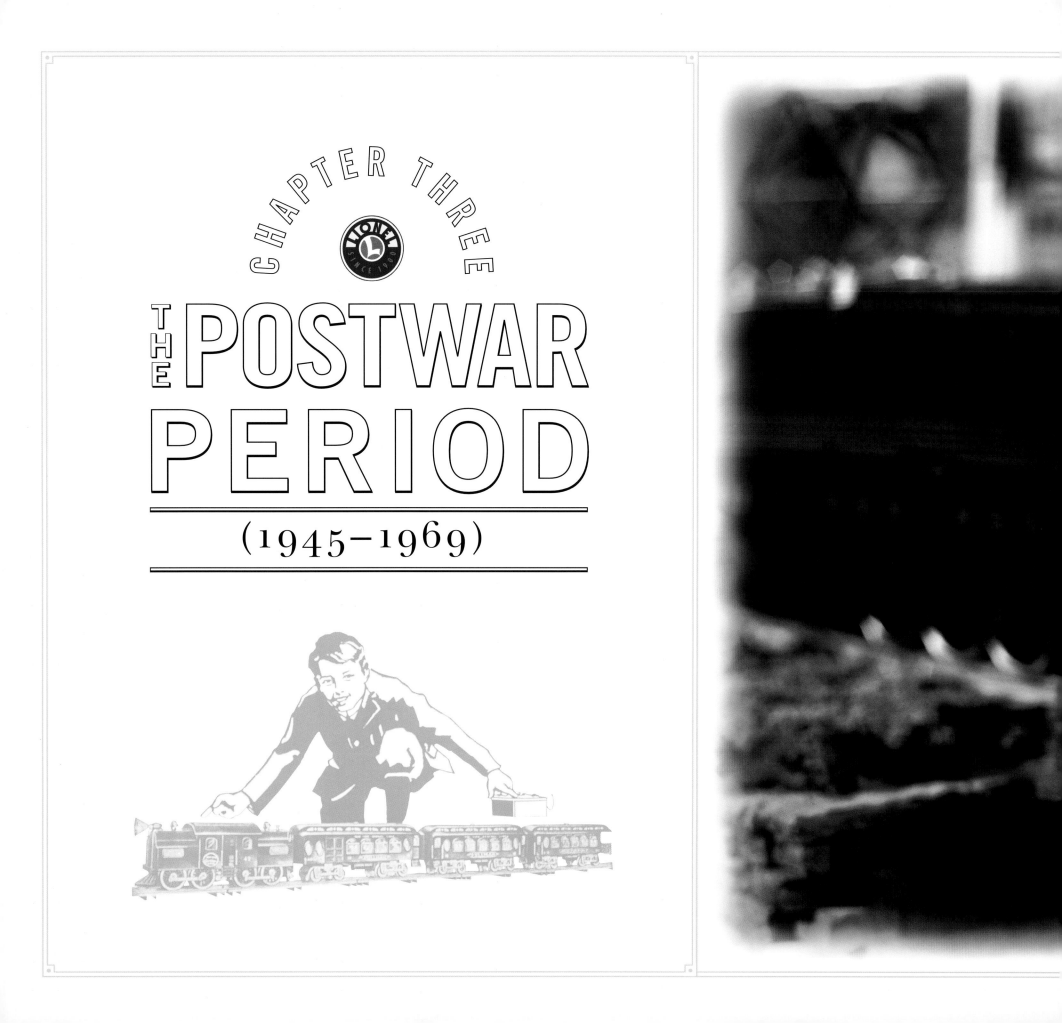

America's joy at the end of World War II was surpassed only by the national desire to return to normal life as quickly as possible. This included the return of a variety of toys that had been absent for the duration of the war. No new electric trains had been manufactured after 1942, even though some older stock had been available for some of that time. War demands had turned the toy companies into part of the manufacturing colossus that enabled the Allies to defeat the Axis powers.

The end of the war came in 1945, but too late for full production to be commenced in time for Christmas. Lionel responded as the great innovator that it was by cobbling together a train set that made use of older production items for which parts were already in existence or could be made without too much difficulty. The set was not one of Lionel's best, but it helped fill the void until the assembly lines could be returned to what they did best: making toy trains.

The 1945 special set marked the first use of operating knuckle coupler trucks, setting the tone for the realism that was to dominate the early postwar years. This simple innovation caught Lionel's main competitor, the A.C. Gilbert Company, flatfooted. Gilbert had no new plans for a realistic coupler truck; instead, it offered a modification of its prewar pressed-steel link-and-pin coupler truck, which by 1945 had become a dated design.

The first year in what train collectors refer to as the postwar period was 1946. Both Lionel and Gilbert had been preparing for this moment even as the war wound down. Many high-level planning-session documents reveal that the toy train aspect of these companies was never really completely dormant. It seems both giants knew that peacetime in the United States would bring back another kind of conflict—pitched battle over the next generation of toy train buyers and their children.

Realizing what was at stake, both Lionel and Gilbert knew that it was important to make a good impression on the train-starved consumer for Christmas 1946. Gilbert revealed the most startling change: a total abandonment of their O gauge line and the advent of what they termed "S" gauge trains, designed to run on two-rail track. This single change divided the train market, completely separating 0 gauge and S gauge collectors. No longer was there compatibility between the products of the rival companies, as there had been before the war. Marx, the distant third-place holder in the hierarchy of American electric train manufacturing, decided to continue manufacturing their trains to run on three-rail O gauge track, but determined to keep its focus on cheaper, mass-market products. This left Lionel as the

pages 6o–6r: The No. 2332 GG-1 locomotive is a true model-railroad classic. It was first offered in 1947 and then on and off in various forms until 1963. The GG-1 sums up everything that was best about the trains of the postwar period—their power, styling, quality, and romantic allure. One cannot say enough about the impact this engine had on the postwar market. This 2332 was the first GG-1 offered and is still the most common due to the large number produced; later models are hard to find and are collector's items. The expense of later GG-1s limited their sales distribution. They were top-of-the-line sets, and the lucky boy who had one was the envy of all his neighborhood friends.

above: While it looks like a prewar design, the No. 221 loco was really made in 1946–1947. Made in both black and gray, it copies vaguely the Dreyfus-designed Hudson that the New York Central Railroad had been running before the war. The 221 had a short run, but enough of them were made that it is not a rare item today.

opposite: The No. 2333 New York Central was the first issue of the NYC F-3 diesel loco. It was designed to appeal to the East Coast toy train fan base, while the Santa Fe was designed to capture the West Coast market. The NYC never sold as well as the Santa Fe and was dropped in 1954, while the Santa Fe appeared in one form or another up until 1966.

above: The No. 128 newsstand was a fascinating accessory manufactured between 1957 and 1960. Making use of the new (at the time) Lionel vibrating motor, the noisy accessory featured a dog that chased its tail around a fireplug, a newsboy hawking papers in front of the stand, and a newsstand dealer moving about in the stand. The item was interesting to watch, but since it didn't interface with the trains it was not destined to be an all-time sales record breaker. Even as late as the early 1970s, some larger Lionel dealers still had 128s for sale.

country's largest manufacturer of complete three-rail lines.

The achievements of 1946 were spectacular. Both Lionel and Gilbert finally released products featuring the long-awaited locomotive smoke. Lionel chose a cumbersome design that required a special lamp with a dimple to heat up a special pill. The resulting suspension of particles was blown out the engine's miniature smokestack. Gilbert tried a different approach: a special bellows connected to a heater unit with its own motor, located in the tender, heated a special liquid that provided a much greater volume of smoke and a pleasing *choo-choo* sound. The tender was connected to the loco by a rubber hose leading to the engine's smokestack. There is evidence to suggest that both companies had worked out the smoke feature during the prewar period.

Also making an appearance were some old favorites from the prewar days: the bascule bridge, the coal loader, the log loader, and the magnetic crane. Lionel's 1946 trains carried the prewar whistle system, but Gilbert did not have a system that was as convenient or that did not violate one of Lionel's patents. No Flyer engines in 1946 made any sound other than the choo-choo. While this may seem like a small issue, it was a big deal to the legions of small boys and their fathers who expected a toy train to whistle as it wound its way around the family Christmas tree.

And Lionel had yet another innovation. By using various radio receivers tuned to different frequencies, it was able to offer the first train to operate entirely by electronic control. Although limited to one train set, the concept was designed to be expanded. Unfortunately, due to the fussy nature of the radio receivers and the limited number of items available to use with the set, it was destined to became a dead end for Lionel.

The 1946 catalog contained some other unusual items as well. The No. 38 water tank used a pump and real water to simulate the filling of a locomotive tender. This item was not destined for success either because the accessory leaked and became clouded with various deposits from the water. A new steam turbine was introduced, and went on to become an all-time Lionel favorite; though it went through several design changes, it was offered in the catalog until 1955. Finally, the catalog presented a scale Hudson set modified for smoke, but this locomotive was never produced.

Regardless, the 1946 catalog was the first real train catalog since 1942, and it was widely distributed. Lionel even arranged for it to be included as an insert in *Liberty* magazine. For a public that had not seen toy trains in years, the 1946 line, even though it was an assortment of old and new concepts, was a sure sign that life in America was returning to normal. This illusion was soon dispelled, however, as political events in Europe turned former allies into enemies and the Cold War commenced.

As political tensions increased, so did the competition for the loyalty of American train

buyers. In 1947 Lionel released a classic, the operating milk car. This fascinating car, in which a miniature milkman delivers milk cans to a trackside platform, has remained in almost continuous production in one form or another ever since. Designed by an outside inventor, the milk car was snapped up by Cowen's company and soon became closely identified with Lionel. The milkman must have been quite strong, as the car sometimes ejected a can across the platform—the equivalent of hurling a five-gallon (9L) metal milk can fifty feet (15m)! The remote-control set again appeared in the

catalog, adorned with oddly placed atomic symbols meant to reflect the advanced scientific principles used in its creation. Its high cost and complexity, however, guaranteed that it would not be as popular as the milk car.

As toy train production gradually returned to prewar levels, the public's fascination with these metal playthings continued to grow. It soon became the norm for the average family to have a train set up at Christmastime, if not all year round. If the family had no boys, Dad bought them for the girls. Lionel was quick to pick up on this trend, and it began including

above left: This prewar Chemcraft set was one example of Lionel's numerous efforts to diversify beyond toy train production. The sets never sold as well as those of Lionel's competitor, A.C. Gilbert (whose reputation was built on scientific toys), but Lionel continued to test the waters of this market until the late 1960s.

above right: *Model Builder* was a Lionel-sponsored magazine that for a time became the country's premier O gauge railroading publication. The successor to *The Lionel Magazine*, *Model Builder* became a sounding board for new ideas and helped make railroading a national pastime. The cover here depicts what boys of all ages dreamed about in 1946: getting a new Lionel train.

Mom and Sis in ads promoting the wholesome fun enjoyed by the family who had Lionel electric trains. Dad and the boys were still the dominant image, but Mother and the girls stood by looking on approvingly or supportively. The women of the house were never shown running the trains in these early postwar catalogs, but they were always present.

Despite increasing tensions in Germany and Eastern Europe, Americans glowed with a renewed self-confidence, and this feeling was reflected in the Lionel catalogs for 1947 and 1948. A flurry of new offerings appeared; most of them went on to become classics. In 1948 Lionel offered the GG-1 and F-3 diesel. The GG-1 was the first postwar electric-style model locomotive. Before the war, the electric-type loco had been an important seller in the tinplate line due to the extensive electrification of railroads in the eastern United States. The die-cast model of the GG-1, the most ubiquitous electric loco ever to grace the American rails, continued that tradition of success into the postwar period. Its sleek art deco look, created by industrial designer Raymond Lowey, made it an instant winner and a perpetual favorite among train enthusiasts.

The GG-1 passenger train was in use on the country's Amtrak railroads until the 1980s, when it finally gave up the ghost, due in part to the use of PCB coolants in its transformers and cracks in its cast truck frames. The GG-1 passenger train holds the record for longevity. Several examples are preserved today at various railway museums around the nation, and they look every bit as sharp as they did decades ago, when they first rolled out of the Baldwin locomotive erection shops.

The Lionel model made use of high-quality die-castings, and although the body was shortened to negotiate the sharper O gauge turns, it still entranced every little boy and grown man who saw it in the toy shop window. Unfortunately, the first model had several peculiarities.

First, for all its weight it was really underpowered—with only one motor—and tended to slip when pulling any sizeable train. Second, its innovative horn, designed to copy the original, emitted a grating, rattling sound that did not endear it to the mothers of young train enthusiasts.

Third, the first GG-1s were painted black instead of the correct dark Brunswick green of the Pennsylvania Railroad, though this was later corrected. These incorrectly colored models are very difficult to find today. Finally, the gold pinstriping was very unstable. The color seemed to

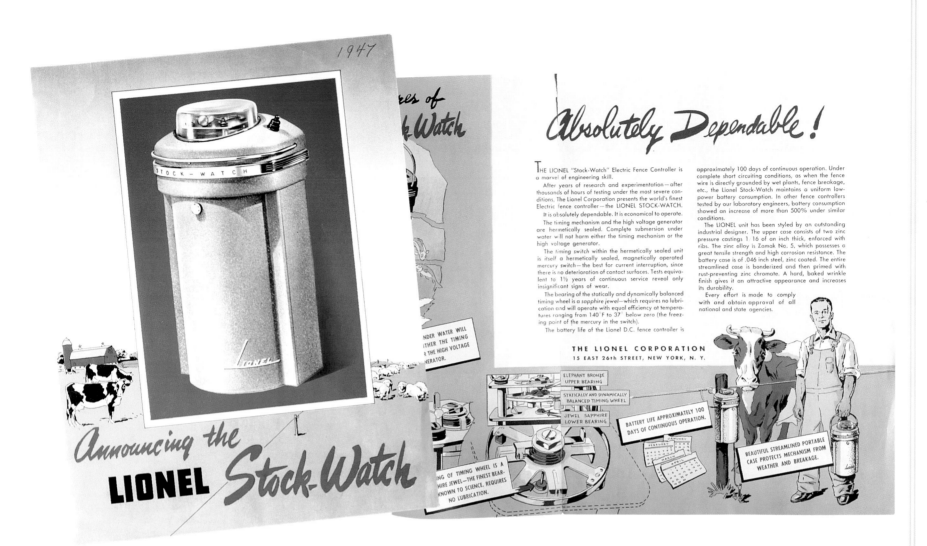

fade whether or not the item was handled heavily, and few models found today still have the original cat's whiskers design intact.

The postwar period brought not only a retooling of the GG-1, but also an entirely new diesel: the F-3. Cowen had loved steam locos from his boyhood, so he resisted producing diesels as long as possible. By the late 1940s, however, realism had become all-important to model railways and there was no denying that the real railroads were marching steadily toward complete dieselization. The end of the steam

loco was in sight, and it was time to produce a toy diesel.

Lionel selected a real winner in the F-3. Before the war, real locomotive manufacturers had been steadily entering the diesel market with a bewildering array of prototypes. The F-3, a well-designed and finely engineered machine, was the first diesel to gain widespread acceptance, and it went on to become an icon of American railroading. Through clever negotiations with General Motors and the Santa Fe and New York Central railroads, Lionel was able to

split the costs of tooling for its model, which was expensive for its day. In return the GM logo was placed on every loco; Santa Fe and NYC versions were produced for only the first several years. The toy locomotive was not only a masterpiece of engineering and technical achievement, but also approached scale realism. To many collectors, the original F-3 represents the zenith of Lionel postwar designs.

The original catalog illustration for the F-3 has caused controversy among collectors. Since the catalog was created before a prototype F-3

opposite: The No. 622 Santa Fe switcher was a Lionel classic featuring a die-cast frame and automatic ringing bell. It was designed to give the Lionel postwar line a modern switching engine. It was manufactured from 1949 to 1950 and was later introduced as No. 623 without the annoying bell. Many layouts of the postwar years featured a Santa Fe switcher in the freight yard.

above: One of the oddest examples of a nontrain product designed by Lionel was the "Stock-Watch" cattle fence controller, released in 1947. This device electrified farm fencing in order to keep cattle penned in. Apparently, there are a few examples still in use, even though it wasn't an overwhelming success. This is the original ad sheet.

was available for the artist to copy, an HO model was used. The resulting picture looks for all the world like an enlarged Varney. (Varney was a pioneering manufacturer of HO trains, an example of which probably served as the model for the artist's depiction of the O gauge F-3.) The colors were also problematic. In real life, Santa Fe used silver and crimson on its F-3 passenger units. The engine in the catalog, however, has a definite black tone to it, which has given rise to the speculation that Lionel might have produced a prototype in black and red. Another explanation may be that, given the limitations of the color printing process of the day, the artist may have tried to use the darker color to indicate a reflective silver surface and was unable to correctly duplicate the reflective nature in the catalog, instead ending up with a shimmering black-toned diesel.

The Santa Fe was the more popular of the two initial offerings. Perhaps the striking paint scheme caught the fancy of the buyer in much

the same way that the attractive colors of the actual train appealed to real-life rail travelers. The Santa Fe went on to become the best-selling diesel ever offered by Lionel. Through intensive advertising, it also became closely identified with the Lionel name; it was the most asked-for toy train of the time.

In 1949 Lionel followed up with a scale model NW-2 switcher with ringing bell, which was in actuality an improvement of a similar model marketed by a small rival firm, General Models Corporation. The GMC switcher was all die-cast and featured a troublesome reverse unit designed to circumvent Lionel's patents on the E-unit, which was the leader in its field for consistent operation. The Lionel model was the first loco to use Magne-Traction. Locomotives that featured Magne-Traction had magnetized driving wheels that gave the engine a better purchase on the tracks—especially useful in navigating uphill grades and the like.

While Lionel's NW-2 switcher was modestly priced and was needed to fill out the firm's line of locomotives, it did not enjoy the response the F-3 had. It was successful enough, however, to end any threat from GMC. Painted in a black-and-white lettered Santa Fe scheme, it was rather drab and plain as it trundled about the layout doing yard work. Early photos of the factory layout from 1949 show an odd light-colored switcher parked near the round house. Research has shown that this was a GMC model repainted by the engineering department as a study model for Lionel's own design.

Lionel also introduced the operating cattle car in 1949. This car seems to have found its way onto most home layouts, even though the cattle often "balked" going into the car. They sure looked good milling around the pen, though, and the cattle car became the number-two-selling operating car of the time.

These successes prompted Gilbert to bring out its own version of the Santa Fe in 1950—a model of the real-life rival to the F-3, the PA-1 made by the American Locomotive Company. Up to this time, Gilbert had been content to offer a wide variety of sets with few innovations. The company's prewar ³⁄₁₆-O gauge line had been a precursor to the S gauge trains offered after the war, and there were a variety of locomotives available to use in sets, from the small Reading Atlantic to the massive Union Pacific Northern to the odd Nickel Plate Road eight-wheeled switcher. But this did not mean that Gilbert's American Flyer was resting on its laurels. In one important move, the company improved its

1947

1948

opposite top: Introduced in 1946, the No. 38 pumping water tank lasted only two years. It was an overly complicated device that simulated the filling of a tender by the apparent dropping of the water level in a double walled see-through tank using a crude pumping action and colored dye tablets. The result was not very convincing and since leakage was a problem the item was dropped in favor of a non-pumping No. 30 tank. Few of the pumping tanks survived, and even fewer still operate correctly. Water and electrical trains were not a good mix and Lionel never made another accessory of this type.

opposite bottom: The Madison-type cars were carried over from prewar production and were made from 1946 to 1950 in various forms. They were among the first items made of the early phenolic plastics that Lionel was experimenting with before the war. They are among the most sought-after cars since they disappeared during the Korean War period, never to reemerge. One rumor says their dies were scrapped accidentally; another says that due to the material's fragile nature (they were called one-shot cars—one drop and they were shot), Lionel turned to other materials to make passenger cars after 1950 and the Madison dies could not be modified to accept this change. Whatever the truth, they are classics that span both the pre- and postwar periods.

above: Catalog covers from 1947 (top) and 1948 (bottom) featured the No. 675 and No. 671 locos, respectively. These new locomotives contained many features, such as whistles and smoke, that appealed to the train buyers of the time and both sold very well.

smoke unit. The new Hudson was also available with a freight set, which sold well and today is fairly common. Also offered was the Union Pacific 027 set, often referred to as the Lionel anniversary set even though the company never advertised it as such. The striking yellow and gray paint of the Alco FA-2 unit, along with matching cars, makes it among the most colorful sets of the early postwar period.

After the war, people seemed to believe that America had returned to its normal peacetime state, that things were just as they had been before Pearl Harbor. Unfortunately, however, this was wishful thinking—the social conditions and political situations created by the Second World War guaranteed that American society would never return to that idyllic state. By 1950, it was becoming apparent that the old rules, style, and attitudes were no longer valid.

The greatest changes were to be seen on the political front. For a brief period after the war, due to the monopoly the United States had on atomic weapons technology, the country seemed to be in a position to exert its influence across the globe unchecked. This was temporary, however, as the U.S.S.R. was hurrying to catch up in the first leg of the so-called arms race. Also, there was a frustrating political stalemate; the United States and the Soviet Union—the superpowers, as they soon became known—were in an ideological battle, with international hegemony at stake. And while the atomic bomb played a major role in this situation, it did not give the United States the upper hand in negotiations—even during the period before the Soviet Union became an atomic power.

By 1950, the U.S.S.R. had spread its military might across half of Europe. Churchill's Iron Curtain speech in 1946 had called the world's attention to the fact that the Soviet Union had been systematically creating a series of satellite states to protect itself from future invasion from the West. This new empire was based not upon democratic politics, but on the monolithic

a b o v e : The 1949 catalog cover shows the postwar family as envisioned by Lionel. The family does things together and window-shops in their Sunday-best outfits. Dad and Junior are the most excited about the new 1949 Lionel products, and Sister and Mom look on approvingly. It was a time of immense promise in the United States.

o p p o s i t e : Introduced in 1948, the New York Central F-3 diesel was one half of Lionel's initial entry into the field of diesel power. The NYC appeared in various numbers until 1955, when it was dropped from the line. With its drab color it never had the sales appeal of its Santa Fe sister loco, but East Coast modelers grabbed them up. Its large sales volume makes it a true postwar classic, with a lightning-bolt paint scheme that faithfully duplicated the original.

smoke units by moving them into the loco itself, creating huge volumes of smoke and a pleasant sound effect—and synchronizing smoke emissions with the choo-choo sound. Similarly, Lionel responded to problems with its own smoke by doing away with the smoke bulb and developing a new type of heater that became the firm's standard unit for the rest of the postwar period.

The year 1950 marked Lionel's fiftieth anniversary. The company issued a special advance edition of the catalog for dealers that had a gold cover. The consumer version of the catalog was less ostentatious and featured a steam passenger train on the cover.

There were also interesting things between the covers, including a revised Hudson, the first since prewar times to be released with the Madison passenger cars. Even though it had less trim, this loco, Lionel's gift to consumers in 1950, looked great, and, better yet, featured the

political views of the Russian Communist Party. This situation was further complicated by the presence of Joseph Stalin, a forceful yet enigmatic and unpredictable leader. Then in 1949 the world learned that the Soviets had developed their own atomic bomb; the Cold War had begun in earnest. Instead of returning to pre-Depression idylls, the United States became consumed by fear and uncertainty.

In the midst of all this, toy trains must have seemed like a stabilizing link with prewar American society, a connection to the comforts of the past. But social change at home and abroad threatened to undermine this, and the toy train giants were once again forced to respond creatively in order to maintain their profits and market positions.

The first big blow, not only to the toy train manufacturers but to the hobby industry as a whole, was the introduction of reliable home television sets. Before the war, televisions had been scientific novelties, but now they were beginning to become household items. Regular programming was soon developed, and America's love affair with the television began. Unfortunately, this fascinating new opportunity

above: The Lionel milk car came with a stamped tin platform (shown here), onto which the milk cans could be unloaded. Platforms like this one, surrounded by miniature workers, were a common sight on many postwar Lionel layouts.

right: The No. 2023 twin-unit Union Pacific Alco FA-1 diesel was produced in 1950 with both a freight and passenger set. The passenger set is often referred to by collectors as the fiftieth anniversary set, though it was never listed as such by Lionel. The very first diesels featured gray noses and are among the most unusual items Lionel ever produced.

for family fun competed directly with model railroading, taking away the precious leisure time that was required to build a miniature empire of the rails in the living room.

Both Lionel and Gilbert jumped on the TV bandwagon early by developing fifteen-minute programs (predecessors of the infomercial). Lionel came on strong with *The Lionel Club House*, in which sports was the main topic of discussion and the Yankee Clipper, Joe DiMaggio himself, was emcee. Lionel names and products figured prominently in the show, with the young audience all wearing Lionel Club shirts. Gilbert offered two different shows: *The Roar of the Rails*, which featured Grandpappy telling Junior about real-life railroad adventures and using American Flyer trains to act them out, and the more famous *Boys Railroad Club*, where Herc and the gang entertained real railroad men with their basement Flyer layout. After these infomercial shows had run their course, both companies embarked on the use of regular television commercials throughout the rest of the 1950s, although Lionel certainly was the more prolific, both in terms of the quantity and types of ads. Both companies also made sure that its trains were featured on as many other television shows (for instance, game shows) as possible; often, whole episodes were built around them.

Lionel products were also used in movie shorts of the 1950s. One such ad was a Joe McDoaks short that featured the harried Mrs. McDoaks seeking marriage advice from a radio marriage counselor, Mr. Agony, about her husband's obsession with Lionel trains, which ran through the house and even delivered food to the table.

Television, however, wasn't the only challenge for toy makers that arose out of the increasingly technological postwar age. Americans were becoming more and more mobile as they became car owners; with highways crisscrossing the nation, not only were railroads feeling the pinch, but people were not as likely to stay home building and playing with model railroads.

But the real menace—the growing influence of the smaller HO train lines—was only slowly being perceived by Lionel and the other manufacturers. The HO gauge, which had been around since before World War II, was viewed as a novelty for the true craftsman who wished to display his mechanical skill by building what seemed like impossibly tiny electrical trains. Lionel had not opted to try HO before the war, but had instead joined the OO trend, which petered out when HO items became more widely available. Gilbert had offered a ready-to-run HO set in the late 1930s, but it was AC-powered and not exactly a jewel of engineering, and though it sold well enough, Gilbert did not expand the line greatly before the war.

Crude kits and expensive motors that were difficult to work with dominated the HO field.

Gordon Varney changed all that. As pioneer of American HO, he offered cheaper and better-designed kits and ready-to-run items that performed as well as they looked. The American public was captivated by these miniaturized trains. They did not smoke or blow a whistle, but they were small and could be operated on a card table. This was ideal for postwar America; mobility had increased and housing was in short supply, so a smaller train system seemed to make perfect sense. Lionel attempted to offset this challenge by offering increasingly more innovative and ingeniously designed accessories and options to entice the buyer away from the smaller trains. This policy worked for a while, but HO would eventually have to be squarely dealt with—that is, adopted or emulated—by all manufacturers.

The worsening Cold War soon gave rise to the Korean War, a conflict that many Americans did not understand and that had to be fought with what to some seemed like too many restrictions. To better allocate resources for the war, President Truman reactivated the Office of Price Stabilization to set caps on consumer pricing and otherwise manage the economy. Lionel boxes suddenly began sporting the OPS sticker. Korean War demands also dried up the sources for magnetic materials, so some locos issued during the Korean War were made without the popular Magne-Traction feature. The whole episode had an unsettling effect on the American mindset, especially when people realized that having the atomic bomb did not in any direct way help the situation in Korea, which had developed as a conventional conflict under the auspices of the United Nations. Furthermore, trying to maintain its edge, the United States had developed and exploded the first hydrogen bomb in the Pacific in 1952. This may have been meant to reassure the U.S. public, but in fact its impact was just the opposite—it only served to fuel the now spiraling arms race between the United States and the Soviet Union.

The year 1952 was another transition year for Lionel. There was a slowly emerging emphasis on new names and colorful paint jobs. It seemed that the public was no longer interested in the drab colors of the prewar era. The Santa Fe started this trend, but from 1952 on Lionel made color a key part of its marketing plan. Between 1952 and 1953, we see the first of the 6464 boxcars, one of the earliest collectible series from Lionel, and the slow emergence of diesel engines as the real conveyor of attractive colors: the Western Pacific F-3 in silver and orange, the C&O switcher in blue and yellow, the Rock Island diesel in red and black, and

boxcars colored orange, silver, blue, and green. The color explosion had begun, and Lionel's market share climbed each year despite the Cold War and the HO lines nibbling at Lionel's heels. Each year, Lionel catalogs became larger and larger, and the train sets more extensive, with offerings in all price ranges.

Around this time, discount marketing began to emerge as a threat. The idea of slashing list prices, taking less profit in order to sell more product, was not a common marketing concept in prewar America. After the war, however, with many consumers looking to spend pent-up earnings, the practice soon spread. Much like the

growth of price clubs in the 1990s, discount marketing was creeping across the landscape in the 1950s and changing the nation's buying habits forever.

Discounters did not necessarily offer everything carried in a particular catalog, but what they did offer came at a reduced cost, which meant considerable savings for the consumer. People now sought out savings in train-set purchases much as they sought out savings in every other product area. Depending on where they were located, the smaller purveyors of Lionel trains began to suffer drops in sales. To offset this alarming trend, Lionel adopted a confusing and perhaps damaging strategy beginning with the 1955 catalog: it stopped listing set prices. The idea was that the consumer would go to his train retailer to see the set and make the deal. To pacify the large toy train dealers, Lionel offered special uncataloged sets they could carry that were unique to

them; it was also hoped that this would help keep the small hobby shops in business by removing the large retailers from direct competition.

In 1954, American Flyer won a quarter of the train market, and although this was nowhere near Lionel's share, it was Gilbert's best year ever. After 1954, American Flyer train sales began a slow but steady decline, despite new products and innovative accessories. Lionel, however, had several more good years, although its sales peak had been in 1953. Lionel introduced most of its key collectibles in these years, including numerous operating cars and accessories. Sadly, all this came with a slow shift away from the high-quality designs advocated by Cowen to more cost-effective products created for ease of assembly and to generate higher profits.

Introduced in 1954, the widely admired Lackawanna TrainMaster diesel was the first major unit to make use of pressed-steel rather

than a die-cast floor. Although magnificent in both looks and operation, it marked the start of a trend away from die-casting that would continue for the rest of the postwar era. Gilbert tried to meet the challenge of Lionel's TrainMaster by adding a dummy unit (an unpowered locomotive) to their existing GP-7 loco and offering this mix-and-match product to its S scale customers.

The year 1954 also marked the release of Lionel's new magnetic gantry crane, the final offering of the workhorse NYC F-3, and a continuation of the company's policy of more color and greater variety, made manifest through a new paint job on the NW-2 switcher (a striking blue and orange for the Seaboard model) and the green and gray livery of the Southern F-3. Many boxcars were scattered throughout the 1954 catalog, and the cover, showed a boy and his dad beaming over a spread of Lionel locos, is an all-time favorite. In an effort to offer a lower-

---

above: The inside front page of the 1949 catalog featured a No. 675 steam loco with all the quality features pointed out for the reader, along with an explanation of why Lionel trains were the world's best.

opposite: Another entry in the broad array of Lionel flatcars, the No. 6817 (1959–1960) with Allis Chalmers tractor and scraper was designed to appeal to the young boy's endless fascination with heavy machinery. This particular version is the 6424-11 red-molded frame with the common version of the tractor; other, much rarer versions of both flatcar and load exist and are considerably more valuable.

priced diesel, Lionel issued the F-3 with a single motor instead of dual motors for the first time. By the mid-1950s, as the toy market continued to change, price was becoming a major issue.

In another move designed to expand Lionel's product base and utilize all its manufacturing facilities, the company again considered product lines unrelated to trains. One famous excursion into the nontrain realm was the ill-fated Linex stereoscopic camera line. This idea revisited late-Victorian-era photographic technology that produced a dual-image slide that, when viewed through a special device, resolved into a three-dimentional image. A low-end entry into an already saturated market, Lionel's camera failed miserably. Lionel's other new venture was the Airex fishing tackle line. There was great interest in fishing among Lionel management, and the Airex line was one of the few nontrain products Lionel actually made money with. The name Airex was featured on billboards and box-cars in the train line in the mid- to late 1950s.

For the remainder of the decade, the cost cutting at Lionel continued unabated, along with the unfulfilled search for the ideal second line of products. There was further redesign of the Lionel motor trucks, and the F-3's drive unit went through several design changes to facilitate assembly and eliminate some applied trim. Eventually, the entire motor truck assembly was redesigned to reduce trouble with the motor and gearing. Unfortunately, these changes altered the F-3 enough to make the redesigned models seem cheap when compared to the earlier versions.

In 1955 the continuing march toward more efficient (and less expensive) production continued with the introduction of a new version of the NW switcher. The old model had a die-cast floor and separate motor. The new design had a stamped sheet-metal floor and used relatively soft aluminum as the main metal in its assembly, which led to quicker deterioration than in the old models. Young operators' constant forward-

top: The No. 3459 dump car was in production from 1946 to 1948, and was later renumbered and run until 1955. The aluminum-bin version is very rare and was only used on the first examples. Some early Lionel publicity photos show a similar car lettered B&O, but all known examples are stamped Lionel Lines. This was a very popular car, and was likely to be found on the average train layout. Only the aluminum version is uncommon.
above: The No. 3656 operating cattle car was produced in several forms between 1949 and 1955. It was supplied with a corral in which pesky cattle milled about, sometimes needing prodding to board the car. It was one of the best-selling Lionel operating freight cars of the time.
opposite: The striking cover of the 1952 catalog—one of the most memorable Lionel ever produced—contained a wonderful image of a very happy boy and all the types of trains Lionel was making that year.

reverse action would cause the soft metal to loosen up and allow the armature to shift in alignment, making the motor jam in one or both directions. This was one of the mysteries of the age—many a father could not understand why his son's train would run well in one direction, only to grind along in the other. Unfortunately for owners, Lionel was quite pleased with this cheaper power truck motor. It was easier to produce and assemble into an engine, and since replacement of the engine was the main repair remedy in the end, it meant increased business for the company. Lionel decided to use these motors in the rest of the lower- and medium-priced diesel-type locomotives from this time forward.

In 1955, Lionel finally responded to the Gilbert GP-7 loco by issuing its own version. Lionel's well-received Geep, as it was affectionately called, had a sheet metal frame and could be produced in fully detailed or stripped-down versions, depending upon marketing needs. At least the Geep was designed to use Lionel's better motor truck design, which made it a reliable puller and a popular piece. In general, Lionel continued to offer higher-priced premium sets and remained on its quest for a low-cost winner. In 1955 Lionel released the famous Congressional passenger set: a GG-1 loco with matching Pennsylvania Railroad aluminum passenger cars. Also offered were a GG-1 freight and the favorite among Lionel enthusiasts, the

spectacular Virginian TrainMaster, whose striking black and yellow (later blue and yellow) paint with billboard lettering made it one of Lionel's most famous locomotives.

In 1956, Lionel pulled out all the stops and had its best year ever. A huge multimedia advertising campaign was launched. An especially colorful catalog was developed, and special giveaways—the Lionel Lion mask, among others—were produced. In its continuing quest for the ideal low-cost train set, Lionel had redesigned the FA diesel to make use of a sheet-metal floor and the new cheaper power truck. Lionel also introduced an even cheaper locomotive of a new design—an oddly oversized copy of the General Electric forty-four-ton engine. The Lionel model was double the size of the prototype, but by using the new motor it could be put into sets at

a cheaper cost. Offered everywhere, the forty-four-ton GE became the starter set of choice for a whole group of train-buying fathers.

The 1956 catalog again exploded with colors and fascinating new additions to the Lionel line. Consumers could select from trolleys, industrial switchers, GG-1s, TrainMasters in several names, legions of steam locomotives, and page after page of the newest and cleverest operating accessories displayed so as to make train operators want to buy them and take them home that very night.

As usual, Lionel was very careful to keep abreast of real railroad design changes. When the New Haven Railroad contracted General Electric to produce a new electric locomotive to replace its aging fleet of prewar designs, both Lionel and Gilbert were quick to seize upon the

┌───┐
above left: Though a modern accessory, the lift bridge
was a giant model designed to simulate the lift bridges found in
many U.S. railroads in the 1950s. It is enormous, with twin towers and a detailed superstructure that copied in miniature the
complex construction of the originals. This detail features just
one corner of the accessory.

above right: The handsome No. 2245 Texas Special F-3
(1954–1955). A budget-priced version of the original F-3, the
2245 maintained the look and feel of the original but only had
one motor.
└───┘

opportunity to be the first to offer a contemporary design. Lionel was a little more successful;
it had apparently been aware of the New Haven
deal before Flyer was, and Lionel was the first to
have a prototype ready. Lionel's design of the
New Haven EP-5 "Jet" electric—adorned in the
striking McGinnis colors of orange, white, and
black—was both on the cover of the catalog and
inside. The American Flyer version was pictured
only on the back cover of that company's 1956
catalog, almost as an afterthought. Apparently,
by the time Gilbert's model was ready, the cata-

log was too far along to have a new loco inserted
inside.

Though the overall spectacular sales in 1956
seemed to indicate that the train-buying public
had not yet been turned away from trains by
anything the Cold War and other social changes
had thrown at 1950s America, that was about to
change.

Preparations were made for the 1957 line
even before the end of the 1956 buying season.
Lionel was preparing what it believed would be
the greatest change since the introduction of

knuckle couplers and smoke after World War II: a new and superrealistic track system to replace the much-criticized three-rail track.

Gilbert had made this issue one of the main selling points for its two-rail S gauge American Flyer trains. Lionel had been working on the problem for some time, and the reasons for the timing of the new track's release are unclear. Perhaps it took until then to work out all the bugs. Perhaps the quest for a cheaper, more efficient diesel motor had used up too much research and development time. In any

case, here it was. Called Super O to set it apart from any other track on the market, Lionel's new system was unlike anything ever before produced for model trains. Hidden in a realistically shaped tie section that was colored brown and showed great track detail, the copper pickup rail was almost invisible to the eye and allowed Lionel to escape the third-rail criticism it had endured for years. Lionel had such high hopes for the track's success that the cover of the 1957 catalog was used mainly to feature it; there were some new locomotives displayed on the Super

O, but there was no mistaking that the focus was on the track.

Had the Super O been introduced earlier, perhaps the outcome would have been very different for Lionel. By 1957, however, most people had built large elaborate layouts from regular O track, and few wanted to take on the formidable task of re-creating a large layout with Super O. And there were some other concerns that developed as the track remained in use. First, the track connectors, called buss bars, were easy to lose and could under certain conditions work

t o p : Designed to be hung in a toy department, this 1954 ad banner shows the new products for that year. The Lackawanna FM and portal crane are featured, but the real attractions are the special features of the Lionel product: sound, smoke, realistic couplers, and Magne-Traction.

a b o v e : The artist mock-up (left) and completed painting (right) for a page in the 1954 catalog that was produced especially for Lionel himself.

o p p o s i t e : The No. 2432 Clifton dome car represents the Lionel postwar O27 passenger car line. These cars were offered with the lower-priced O27 sets of the postwar period. They were magnificent (but small) models of streamlined railway passenger cars that were in operation on U.S. railroads in the late 1940s. Many of the cars bore the names of towns near the Lionel factory in New Jersey. The most attractive feature of this particular car is the little silhouettes of people illuminated in the windows, which lends the piece a wonderful realism.

themselves loose from the center rail, snagging a truck on a passing train and causing a serious derailment. Second, the switches were of a new design and the motor was not robust enough to stand up to constant abuse from little engineers. The result was a melted and inoperable switch motor. Finally, after prolonged use the center rail itself could wear out rollers and pickups at an alarming rate, requiring more frequent replacement than with normal track.

While track was the biggest news in 1957, the other important item was a new steam loco: the No. 746 Norfolk and Western bullet nose, the first new large steam loco in many years. It was impressive, but in a way it was released too late. The period of the steam loco was over on real American railroads, and even though some roads held on to steam for a time, most of America was dieselized and the release of the 746 did not excite the public as Lionel expected.

Lionel committed one of its most serious marketing blunders in 1957, when it released the pastel-colored girl's train. Lionel was finally allowing girls to have their own trains, offering them in a range of soft and unrealistic colors that management thought would appeal to the youngsters of the time. The company could not have been more wrong—girls wanted to run real trains, not some made-up fantasy on rails. While the girl's train is a collector's item today, it was not popular for the few years it was offered in the catalog and was even ridiculed for its out-landish color scheme.

More importantly, 1957 was the year that Lionel finally decided to take action against the growing threat posed by the HO manufacturers. If they couldn't beat them, Lionel management figured they might as well join them. Since Lionel had nothing on the drawing board, it contracted with the popular Italian HO manufacturer Rivarossi to produce a line for it. Because of the many problems inherent marketing what was essentially a foreign line, the arrangement lasted only one year. However, from 1957 till 1966,

Lionel offered HO trains alongside its regular O and O27 items.

Later in the year, however, there occurred another event that would have a significant impact on the American toy market. In October, the United States—and the entire world—was stunned to learn that the Soviet Union had put the first satellite in orbit around the earth. The impact of *Sputnik* on 1957 America has been described as "panic in the streets," and the nation's focus turned to space and science almost overnight. Trains seemed a reminder of a quaint and distant part of history. The future was up in the skies, not on a set of rails.

Lionel was not prepared for the rapid change of interest, and no toys in the 1957 catalog reflected the new national focus. A.C. Gilbert, while not privy to government secrets, had the good fortune to have included a rocket launcher car in the 1957 lineup. It sold well, and Lionel operators asked why Lionel did not have one as well. From this moment on, space, science, and new technologies dominated the toy train giants as they tried to find their place in the post-*Sputnik* world. Lionel and American Flyer would try many ways to latch on to the new world they saw dawning before their eyes, but in truth none was really successful.

The 1958 catalog cover was garish, to say the least. It was executed in sinister tones of red and featured on its cover a missile launcher surrounded, bizarrely enough, by normal train items. It seems that Lionel wanted to capture the best of both worlds. The featured centerpiece of the catalog was a Lionel version of an Atlas missile launching site with gantry and command bunker. Although it was very realistic, the problem was how to integrate this concept into a toy train layout. The Lionel ad copy implies that the railroad delivered U.S. Navy missiles to the launcher by way of a siding— quite a stretch of imagination to justify such a complicated nonrailway accessory. There was also nothing to aim the missile at; it simply went up into the air and came down some-

where across the neighboring train tracks or village.

Numerous other military-related vehicles were also released. The marine train consisted of a series of flatcars loaded with military vehicles made by the Pyro Plastics Company. The sinister atomic waste car featured evil looking radioactive containers that blinked an ominous red warning. There was even a special Allis Chalmers car that carried a condenser heat exchanger from an atomic power plant, which appeared in the background of one of the catalog pages for the first time. But military and scientific items were not all Lionel offered— there was also a brand new electric-type engine lettered for the Virginian Railroad. This loco was based on a new real-life design, but since

left : The No. 2367 Wabash diesel, produced as an AB unit in 1955, illustrates the variety of real railroad names selected by Lionel for use on its toy trains in the 1950s. The Wabash's colorful gray, white, and blue paint scheme was well known across the United States.

above : An accessory folder featuring the new barrel loader (No. 362) from 1952. The barrel loader accessory was on the market for two years before the No. 3562 operating barrel car was released. Folders such as this one were included with most new train sets to encourage the consumer to buy more Lionel items.

so few were produced—at the time only Virginian had it, though it later passed it on to New Haven and to Conrail—most people had never seen one and could not decide if the loco represented a diesel or an electric.

The HO line was revised by having Athearn, the well known American maker, supply all the products sold under the Lionel HO name. The large offering of 1958 may have looked good on the surface, but it masked a hard fact: train sales were declining, and HO was coming to domi-

nate a larger share of the market at the expense of S and O train sales. Also the year was bad for business in general; there was a recession, and there was some labor unrest.

American Flyer suffered more than Lionel, and 1958 was the last year they would ever field a large catalog and an extensive train line. For Flyer, this was the beginning of the end, for they never recovered from the year's low sales. Lionel, which was a larger company and had greater resources with which to ride out bad

times, seemed to take the year's setbacks in stride and continue planning for 1959. In actuality, the company's confidence was shaken. The only answer, however, was to forge ahead, and Lionel continued its diversification into electronics and other fields unrelated to trains.

To address some of what were perceived to be the root causes of the problems, Lionel came up with a number of changes for 1959. The HO line was to be produced entirely in-house for the first time. To accelerate the

a b o v e : The No. 3530 GM generator car was in production from 1956 through 1958. It was modeled after a real GM power car used to provide railroads with emergency electrical power when track crews were working on the line. The real car was a fully equipped generating station that could provide enough electricity to power a small village in an emergency. The photo does not show the pole and searchlight that were included with the car, making it a fascinating operating piece. When the doors were opened a switch turned on the lights and the rotating fan blade in the car. If the car was hooked up to the light pole, that also came on. Unfortunately, not many Americans in 1956 had ever seen such a car and it was considered an oddity. Even though it was in the line for a number of years, with several minor color variations, it is hard to find a complete example today.

r i g h t : The No. 2328 Burlington GP-7 diesel was produced from 1955 to 1956 and filled the role of medium-priced locomotive for Lionel at that time. It ran well and many other similar GP-type diesels with various names were produced in the postwar period. The silver paint used on the Burlington did not age well, and today a bright example is unusual.

process, Lionel bought the Hobbyline HO Train Company, a firm that had existed since the dawn of the HO era. This line would serve as the base for a redesigned and entirely Lionel-produced HO line.

This approach might have worked; Hobbyline was a reasonably successful brand and was known nationwide. In fact, it had recently gained a large presence in the market, getting its products onto the shelves of several large East Coast department stores for the 1957 Christmas selling season. But Lionel insisted on replacing the existing Hobbyline motor drive with one of its own manufacture, and the Lionel-designed replacement was a disaster. The company never settled on a standard drive system, switching back and forth between O-rings, metal springs, and gears. The motor itself was not one of Lionel's best efforts; other commercially available HO motors were more dependable and more durable. Lionel stubbornly refused to change, however; the name Lionel was thought to be enough to sell the line. The new HO sold well enough for the first few years, until consumers realized the maintenance problems it presented. The A.C. Gilbert company, even with declining sales and an expensive HO line, offered a better motor, derived from the Pittman open frame motor system. Gilbert's failed motors were easily removed and replaced, making repairs simple in most HO lines. With its ever-evolving design, Lionel's system was not so easy to fix.

For both Gilbert and Lionel, the overriding question had to do with their intended market. The two companies saw their HO lines as an extension of their larger train lines and marketed them the same way. Most other HO manufacturers did not emphasize features like horns and whistles, but instead focused on scale design and operational performance. Lionel and Gilbert never understood this subtle difference. Even in the 1960s, Lionel continued to introduce HO whistling tenders and HO diesels with horns.

This was a remarkable engineering feat, but not something that attracted customers; operators were more interested in trains that had realistic paint schemes and ran reliably.

The HO problem haunted the two major toy train manufacturers for quite some time. In the early 1960s, in one attempt to spur interest, Lionel copied some of its O items in HO gauge and offered them to the public. The most famous piece of this nature—the huge father-and-son set—graced the cover of the 1960 catalog. This

above: The No. 51 Navy Yard switcher was one of a series of small industrial switchers Lionel designed as add-on pieces to the train layout. Cheaply priced at about twelve to fifteen dollars, they featured self-power and reversing ability, but oddly enough no working headlight. Made in many different colors and names, they were popular and sold well. Since they were run hard, many are found in poor shape today—the window struts are fragile and were often broken even when handled with care. The Navy Yard model was in production from 1956 to 1957 and is among the easier items to find in this series.

right: The 2321 Lackawanna TrainMaster diesel was a great hit when it was introduced in 1954. It was available with either a gray or a maroon roof and was produced from 1954 to 1956. Its pulling power was legendary and every late-1950s Lionel railway had to have one. The massive size of the locomotive made a great impression on little and big engineers then—and still does today.

set featured an O gauge Santa Fe freight set for Dad and a nearly identical HO Santa Fe set for Son, with the O gauge running on top of the HO by means of a trestle. In the end, however, both companies gave up on HO. Gilbert had many original design items and had been working with the gauge for a long time, but its products were costlier than those of most other manufacturers and its market share was dwindling, along with the company's other fortunes. Finally, in 1964, Gilbert ceased HO production and sold its remaining parts inventory to Polks Model Craft of New York. Lionel soldiered on until 1966, then threw in the towel as well.

In contrast, the O gauge line served the public very well. The year 1959 saw an explosion of new military and space-related cars that would stay on the market through 1964. Among the various missile launching cars was the Minuteman missile launcher, which fired a missile concealed inside a boxcar at a distant target. As fantastic as this may seem, the military had in fact considered developing just such a car, but the device had never moved beyond the planning stage. Even in the fantastic realm of Cold War trains, Lionel still maintained a certain level of realism.

But the company didn't stop there. After the Nautilus became the first submarine to cross under the polar ice pack in 1958, America became very interested in submarine technology. The Lionel submarine featured a rubber band drive motor and could actually be made to dive and surface in water. Of course, one had to be rather creative to incorporate a toy submarine into the average train layout of the period. In a commercial, Lionel showed the sub being used in a nearby fish tank.

After the sea came the air—the release of the Lionel helicopter car was a sales success. Every boy wanted to launch one over his own Lionelville. The helicopter was never as graceful in reality as the Lionel television commercials suggested. One ad even presented the illusion of

top: The No. 60 trolley was an all-time Lionel favorite. Based on the gang car reversing mechanism (which caused the car to reverse direction when the bumper made contact with something on the track), the trolleys trundled around most postwar layouts. In production from 1955 to 1958, the trolley's fascinating action pleased old and young alike. The rarest example featured a motorman silhouette that moved back and forth, the bumper action causing the silhouette to move from one end of the car's interior to the other. This feature was soon dropped, as most people could barely see the effect. Many trolleys were made and they are not difficult to find today, but truly mint examples are uncommon due to the hard use little hands gave them on the Christmas layout.

above: The No. 3662 operating milk car was produced during two time periods, from 1955 to 1960 and from 1964 to 1966. The 3662 was an improved version of the original milk car and was supplied with a tin platform and seven milk cans. This is one of the best-remembered cars of all time. Huge numbers were sold and many still operate today.

sustained hovering flight—talk about truth in advertising (or lack thereof). The chopper often crashed back into the train layout when it came down, and sometimes it didn't come off the launcher at all. Nevertheless, the public loved it, and *Life* magazine created a famous photo spread showing the mass firing of about one hundred Lionel helicopters. *Life* also did a photo spread featuring a diver surrounded by hundreds of Lionel submarines. Sales rose accordingly.

In 1959 Lionel also stepped back in time and released a historic train: the *General* Civil War locomotive and car set. The release of the *General* was tied into two events: the coming anniversary of the Civil War and the popularity of Disney's *The Great Locomotive Chase*, starring Fess Parker of Davy Crockett fame. Tyco HO trains, Marx, and Gilbert all came out with similar sets at the same time, though Tyco seems to have made the first real *General* in HO. Lionel's design was apparently based on an earlier plastic kit that had been released by an HO model kit company. The similarities are quite striking, right down to the decal design on the baggage car. Available as a regular O model and as a deluxe Super O model with extra trim and whistle, the *General* was a moderate sales success for Lionel.

There was a problem, however: how to follow up on a period loco based on a historic event? For the most part, Civil War–vintage trains seem similar in shape and the cars are mostly uninteresting in color and design. Even more limiting, you can't run modern equipment with a period set or use its cars with a modern steam loco. Lionel wanted to capitalize on the

above: The No. 6376 circus car was made from 1956 to 1957. It was an odd car designed to capitalize on the popularity of circuses, many of which were still touring the nation in the 1950s. No specific name was used on the car. It was not a fast seller and may be found fairly easily today. A note of caution: the red lettering and trim is easily damaged if the car is washed.

success of the *General*, but soon realized that the possibilities were rather limited. An operating sheriff and outlaw car tied the *General* into then current cowboy television shows, but the link was weak at best. The *General* became a one-shot wonder. However, all train companies advertised their Civil War trains widely, and judging from the numbers that surface today, these models must have been a welcome success in a declining train market.

Lionel also went beyond the space and technology trend by creating trains that reflected other popular culture interests. For example, the company issued a pickle car in 1960. In a *Dick Tracy* comic strip from around the same time, our hero duked it out with the villainous Flat Top inside a railway pickle car. One can't help wondering if the comic strip inspired Lionel to make the pickle car, or if *Dick Tracy* creator Chester Gould saw Lionel's new toy and incorporated into the strip.

Other Lionel releases seemed simply bizarre, like a mobile missile launcher unit that could be used as a loco. Items such as these were of no interest to avid Lionel collectors and enthusiasts, who disdained their lack of realism.

1960 brought the famous Kennedy/Nixon battle for the presidency. Never one to miss a marketing opportunity, Lionel offered a campaign train in that year's catalog, complete with a whistle stop crowd and candidate. Best of all, included were stickers for both Democrats and Republicans that could be applied to the cars (so as not to damage sales by appearing biased).

opposite: The DL&W work caboose No. 6419 is a handsome car and was very popular during Lionel's postwar golden age. The car originally was issued in a different number with a spotlight, but the non-spotlight version is the one most people remember. It is the perfect companion piece to the Lionel crane car and was made in this number from 1948 to 1950 and 1952 to 1957. It has a die-cast floor and a very detailed superstructure that made it a must-have car for all junior engineers in the 1950s.

below: The No. 6475 pickle vat car was produced from 1960 to 1962, and as Lionel ad copy stated, it was "guaranteed to spice up any train." The odd item was based on the vat car designed to carry pickles and related products on real railroads. It was an older design that was slowly fading from the American railroading scene when the Lionel version was introduced. It can best be described as a novelty car, since many boys had never seen a real one in operation. The car had mixed sales and can be located today without too much difficulty.

above: **The Jersey Central TrainMaster diesel No. 2341 is one of the hardest postwar diesels to find today, as it was only offered in one set in 1956. Many copies and reproductions of it have been made over the years, so it is advisable to consult an experienced train collector before purchasing one.**

opposite top: **The No. 629 Burlington forty-four-ton switcher was one of an odd family of locomotives Lionel produced in the mid-1950s. It was available only in 1956 and was packaged with a passenger set, making it even more unusual. The forty-four-ton-type engines were greatly oversized compared to the prototype engine. Lionel had developed them as low-priced diesels, but they did not enjoy longevity. The Burlington, which is among several railroad names that were produced, is very uncommon, particularly if its silver paint still has a bright finish.**

opposite bottom: **The ZW transformer is another trademark of the Lionel postwar period. Still sought out and used today, the ZW was the only postwar American-made train transformer that could boast of being able to run four trains. It was produced from 1948 to 1966 with modifications. It is still the heart and soul of many modern Lionel layouts. Its characteristic football shape is instantly recognizable by anyone who had Lionel trains as a child during the postwar period.**

But the election was not important to Lionel only because of this one item. With Kennedy's election came a new attitude of hope and progress, and even greater emphasis on science and space technology. The Cold War was still on, but things seemed better, at least for a while. This optimism was reflected in the style and variety of products offered in Lionel's post-election catalogs. The burgeoning interest in technology was shown not only in the train sets but also in an explosion of Lionel science sets and in a line of inventor kits for future scientists. One piece of legislation passed by Kennedy was the National Defense Education Act, which stressed improvement in science and technology in U.S. schools. While this certainly presented an interesting marketing oppportunity, it pushed Lionel farther away from its primary area of manufacturing expertise: trains.

Back in the world of model toys, the advent of the slot car also had a tremendous impact on

train production. Slot car racing had developed in England in the 1950s and was pioneered by the firm Scalextric, which had created a viable racing system to bring the scale racing craze into the home. Slot car racing appeared in the United States near the end of the 1950s and became very popular very quickly. Train manufacturers immediately tried to take advantage of the trend by developing their own lines of slot cars. The most popular scale was originally 1/32, but HO scale cars were soon sweeping the market. Again, both Lionel and Gilbert were slow to react. Gilbert introduced its line, which was approximately 1/32 and used magnetic pickups, in its 1959–1960 catalog. Although the line looked good, it did not work very well. The next year, Gilbert redesigned the whole line as Auto Rama, eventually including pickup trucks and sulkies.

Lionel responded even more slowly, negotiating a deal to distribute Scalextric products in

the United States until 1963, while they geared up for their own production. In 1963 Lionel came out with slot car lines in HO and 1/32. Neither Gilbert nor Lionel enjoyed good sales of their slot car lines, and both soon acquired

reputations for mediocrity. Knowledgeable racing fans knew that almost any other brand was better. Lionel continued to offer racing sets in its catalog through 1966, but never decisively defined its target market or developed a standard product; the company changed the system in some way every year, never a good way to develop customer loyalty.

Throughout the 1960s, Lionel attempted again and again to redefine its mission. The train line changed in many ways, and costs were cut wherever possible. With the coming of Lyndon Johnson to the White House, the word Vietnam entered the everyday vocabulary of the American public. With increasing awareness of this war, public fascination with Cold War military items for the train—and for toys in general—waned. By the time the space age came to an end, Lionel had introduced a bewildering array of these items, including missile launchers, mercury capsule cars, radar cars,

balloon launchers, cannon cars, and even an astronaut cherry picker car. Over time, however, the range of military items shrank, and by 1966 none were to be seen in the O gauge line and only a few in the HO line.

The public's interest in trains had been in decline since the late 1950s. In 1964 Lionel tried to renew interest in the declining O gauge line by reintroducing the 773 Hudson as a replacement for the GG-1, which was dropped after 1963. The Virginian TrainMaster was also reintroduced in 1965. Lionel offered its most unusual space toy in 1964: the giant inflatable spaceship Helios. Attached to a control box by a power cord, this toy was filled with helium and powered by motors that could make it fly around the room. Helios, which made use of an early Mylar-type balloon envelope, was ahead of its time. Although it was successful to a certain point, the helium refill bottles looked like homemade bombs, which made shipping and handling inconvenient, to say the least. Also in 1964, Lionel's catalog featured an enormous and impractical riding boat toy and waterway that could be set up in the backyard.

Although control of the company had since passed out of the hands of the Lionel family, Joshua Cowen was still the spiritual figurehead of the organization. By August of 1965, the eighty-three-year-old founder was visibly ill; at the end of that month he had a stroke, and on September 8 he passed away. The feisty Cowen was gone, but his legacy would live on.

By this time, neither Lionel nor Gilbert was in the best shape. Finding itself losing sales due to a constant decrease in the quality of the Flyer line, Gilbert sought new areas of revenue in every conceivable toy sector. None was successful. Similarly, Lionel attempted to stem the tide by jumping into new marketing trends after the market filled with newcomers whose price and quality put Lionel to shame.

Flyer's last desperate gamble was played out in 1966 with the release of the All-Aboard panel

opposite: The No. 746 Norfolk & Western bullet nose streamliner was produced from 1957 to 1960. It was a copy of one of the last streamlined locomotives built in the United States. Alas, it came too late in the postwar era—steam locos no longer captured the imagination of the public as they had in the early days of Lionel. The 746 is a much-sought-after piece today, but in 1960 many dealers were happy to sell them at a discount just to get rid of them.

above: The No. 2350 New Haven electric loco was modeled after the then-current GE EP-5 engine as developed for the New Haven Railroad. In real life, it was a cutting-edge piece that received much publicity during its testing. The colorful "McGinnis" paint scheme (named after the railroad's then-president) made both the original and the toy stand out. It was very popular when it was introduced in 1956 and it remained in the line through 1958. Although the loco's colorful paint scheme made it an instant success for Lionel, only the body was correctly copied from the original. The trucks used were from the F-3 design and did not reflect the real loco's six-wheel truck arrangement. This oversight did not bother the legions of young and old engineers who eagerly snapped up the 2350 to add to their roster of motive power.

above: The No. 192 operating control tower was produced from 1959 to 1960. It had an interesting action. The control top was illuminated and two operators moved about the inside, apparently going from control panel to control panel. Up on the roof, wind indicators turned to simulate a wind blowing in Lionelville. The tower structure itself was borrowed from the earlier No. 197 operating radar tower (based on Newark, New Jersey's radar tower) and like its predecessor was very fragile. As a result, unbroken examples of the modern-looking tower are rare today.

opposite right: Among the most popular of the many car types Lionel produced during the postwar period was the Bucyrus-Erie crane car. Many different versions exist because every junior engineer needed a "big hook" to put his trains back on the track when derailments occurred. The crane was in production in one form or another from 1946 to 1969.

left: The No. 3360 operating burro crane was cataloged from 1956 to 1957 and was a fascinating accessory. It could be adjusted so that its hoist and cab rotation operated automatically by track-mounted trip devices. The little crane was faithfully copied from the "burro crane" used by real railroads and could even pull several cars. This item is a perfect example of the engineering excellence that went into the best items Lionel made, giving the customer the most value and quality for his hard-earned dollar.

below: The spread from the 1957 catalog featuring the infamous girl's train set. The marketing venture proved one thing: girls did not like pastel trains any more than boys did in 1957 America.

The year 1969 marked the 100th anniversary of the driving of the Golden Spike, symbolizing the completion of the Transcontinental Railroad. Marketing wisdom would seem to dictate that every toy train company should have taken full advantage of this by turning out a memorable line. But such was not the case.

The preceding years had not been kind to larger trains, especially since another challenger had turned up—from Germany. The new and smaller German N gauge took more sales away from the older U.S. manufacturers, of which only Marx and Lionel remained. In 1967 Lionel had merely repeated its 1966 line, and in 1968 it released a folder featuring a train set that consisted of a 2029 loco made in Japan, along with an assortment of cheap cars. The 1969 Gold Spike centennial catalog sported an impressive cover showing a Virginian TrainMaster and a steam loco, but no Virginian was actually made.

Inside, there was a selection of unimpressive sets, the largest of which was a 2029 steamer. The remaining items seemed to be carried over from 1968, the only difference being a reissue of the Sunoco tank car and several 6464 series boxcars from previous years. The scope, vitality, and depth of the past was gone. As a result, 1969 was the last year of existence for the trains division of the original Lionel Toy Corporation.

system, which featured a complete railway layout divided up into panel sections that could be put together and taken apart as often as a child liked. Many saw it as the end of a proud train line, while others felt that if Gilbert had done a better marketing job it could have started a whole new model railroading wave. The line bombed, and in March 1967 Flyer was bought out by Lionel. Its remaining stocks were liquidated to the Lionel dealer network. One closeout sheet listed the now rare Domino sugar hopper for about seventy-five cents each, if bought in quantity. In a huge cleanout sale in the winter of 1967, the complete sets were all sold, along with the loose cars and locos, to the Two Guys from Harrison chain of cut-rate department stores.

After that, you could buy a Flyer Pacific, a searchlight car, a Mobil gas tanker, a crane, and a track cleaner car, all new, all in a special boxed set, for about $9.99.

The end of Gilbert gave Lionel little to rejoice about, however, as sales were slipping and inventories were high. The 1966 catalog was made up of leftover inventory that Lionel wanted to dispose of. Dealers bought these items in large quantities at cut-rate prices, and were still selling many of them into the early 1970s.

above left: The No. 3435 aquarium car was one of the strangest and most interesting cars Lionel ever made. It was designed to simulate the swimming of fish in an aquarium transport car. Through the use of a moving belt and a wavy plastic front panel, the fish seem to swim by when the car is turned on. As fantastic as it seems, the car had a real life prototype used to transport fish to aquariums, but in this case the fish were housed inside tanks in a converted passenger car. This fascinating car seems to have sold well enough during the years it was available (1959–1962). Several minor variations were produced, but the car was fragile enough to make it a sought-after collector's item today.

above right: The Airex fishing tackle company was one of Lionel's few successful nontrain ventures. The subsidiary sold a large variety of fishing equipment and was fairly popular in the 1950s. Lionel even used the name on several pieces of train rolling stock and on miniature billboards. This 1959 Airex catalog is a rarity, as not many people saved fishing tackle catalogs the way they saved train catalogs in 1950s.

opposite: The No. 53 Rio Grande snowplow was an interesting unit manufactured from 1957 to 1960. It used the Lionel industrial switcher–style body and was a fully operating locomotive that could pull several cars. In the initial production run, the Rio Grande was made with the "a" in Grande reversed on the stamping tool, so most feature a reverse letter "a," which is considered the norm. Lionel later fixed the stamping tool and the "a" was correctly positioned. The correctly spelled items are rarites, as very few were actually made this way. Most Lionel units using this body are missing the window struts, as they are very fragile and easily broken.

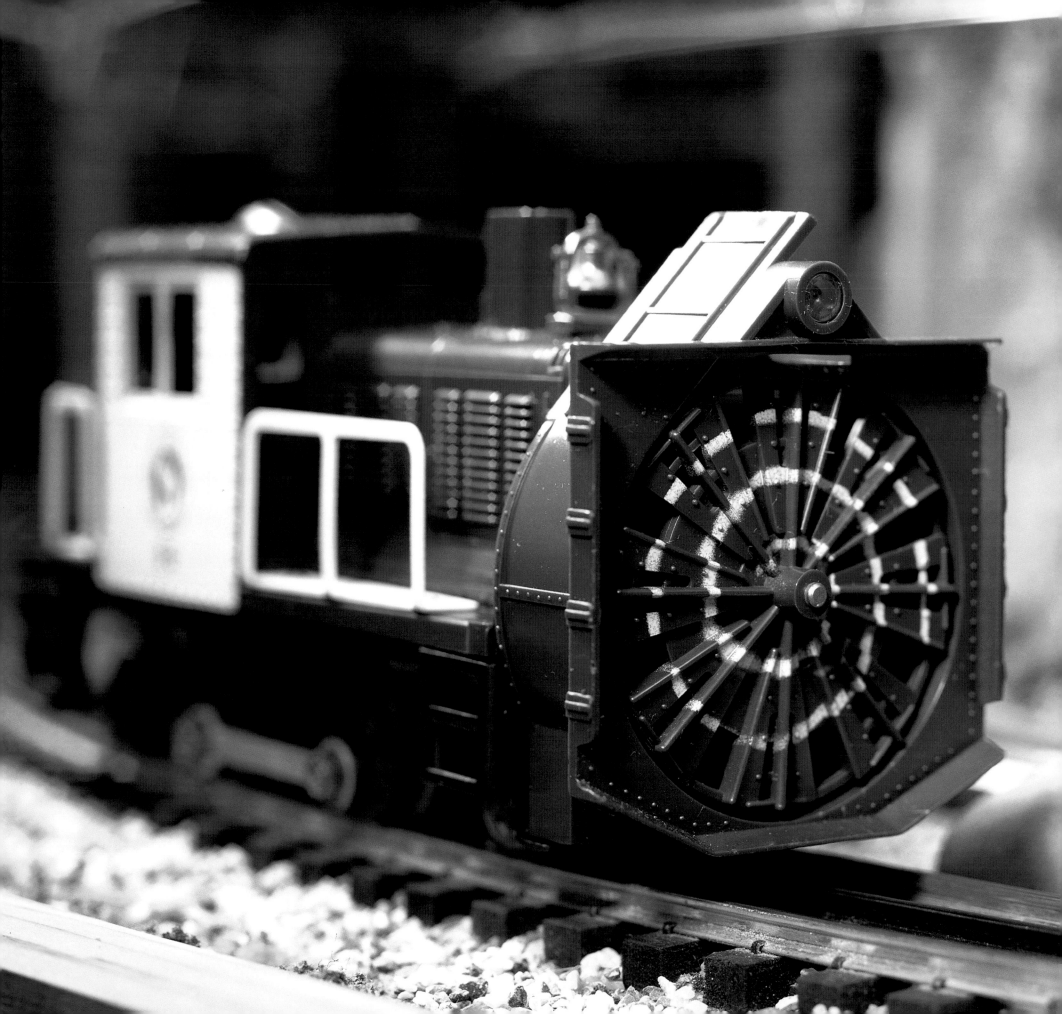

opposite: The No. 58 Great Northern rotary snowplow came along late in Lionel's classic postwar period. Using a modified Navy switcher–type shell, it was first produced in 1959 and remained in production until 1961. Its rotating fan blade was driven by a belt attached to a pulley on top of the motor shaft. Unfortunately, it was very fragile, and few unbroken examples survive today.

above left: The unusual 1957 catalog cover left no doubt about what the big news at Lionel was that year: Super O track. Most of the trains featured were new issues, but they took a backseat to the lines of track coming out of the background toward the viewer.

above right: This 1960 catalog cover from the advance dealers' edition featured similarly dressed fathers and sons peering through a Lionel dealer's window at that year's father-and-son Santa Fe set. The

set was an unusual concept, matching cars in both HO and O gauges (only Lionel manufactured both O and HO trains with the same items in both lines).

above: The No. 68 executive inspection car was based on similar vehicles that most American railroads used to inspect tracks. It featured a newly designed drive system, using drive shafts, that was never used in any other Lionel item. The 68 featured working head- and taillights and was self-powered. Most were painted red and white, but there are rumors of an all-red model. The item sold well and was in production from 1958 to 1961. With a body made of lightweight plastic, it was susceptible to breakage, and its low price of about $12.99 meant that there was little hesitation over throwing out a broken model. This accounts for the scarcity of mint-condition 68s today.

opposite: The No. 52 fire car was a fantasy piece, and Lionel acknowledged it by stating in their service manual that it contained features found on several different types of railroad fire-fighting equipment. The self-propelled unit was based on the No. 50 gang car bump-and-reverse mechanism and featured a red light and a reversing fireman with a deluge cannon. The car was fairly popular and was produced from 1958 until 1961. Its superstructure features a very fragile top that is often broken on surviving models. The photo shows the No. 52 with its companion piece, the No. 3512 fireman and ladder car. The ladder is also very fragile and difficult to find intact; this particular example features the very rare unpainted ladder. Although not designed to be sold together, the two pieces complement each other well. The 3512 featured a red light and revolving fireman all driven by a belt system. The car was in the Lionel line from 1959 to 1961 and was also a fantasy car.

left: The No. 3434 poultry dispatch car was modeled after real cars operating on American railways. The Lionel model was offered in two different runs, from 1959 to 1960 and from 1964 to 1966. It featured an attendant who would open the door and sweep out the car when activated by remote control.

below: The No. 614 Alaska railroad switcher was produced in 1959 and 1960. It was designed to commemorate the statehood of Alaska and was offered in a special set. The switcher itself was modified from normal production switchers with the attachment of a yellow plastic brake and air cylinder piece ahead of the cab on the roof. This addition was used in real life by several railroads. The diesel version is rather uncommon, due to its short production life.

LIONEL

The

Postwar

Period

above: The No. 6557 smoking caboose was made from 1958 to 1959 and featured a working smoke unit, designed to trail a plume of smoke as the caboose was pulled around the track. However, the smoke unit was based around an HO smoke heater element and required a special light bulb wired in series with it to prevent premature burnout. In addition, the volume of smoke produced was erratic. These problems doomed the smoke caboose to a short sales run.

opposite: The Virginian electric was a new-style electric loco made for the Virginian Railroad in the mid-1950s. Model No. 2329 was made from 1958 to 1959. This should have been a winner for Lionel, but it was instead a terrible seller. The main problem was that the Virginian was the only railroad that had this type and few people in other parts of the nation ever had seen one. Also, it looked like a cross between an electric loco and a diesel, and was not pleasing in appearance like the Virginian Trainmaster, which sold very well. Lionel tried everything it could to get rid of back stocks for the next two years. Today the engine is among the must-have pieces for a postwar collection and is not easy to obtain in excellent condition.

opposite: The No. 2358 Great Northern electric used the same body as the 2350 New Haven, painted in Great Northern orange and green. It has the distinction of being the last EP-5 type produced by Lionel during the postwar period and was made from 1959 to 1960. Unfortunately, Lionel took great liberties in passing this off as a Great Northern engine. It is true that Great Northern had electric locos to pull trains through the Rockies, but they never had an EP-5. However, they did have a vaguely similar GE type with multiple wheels. Lionel loosely based their model on this prototype. The Great Northern did not sell well as it was introduced in the twilight years of the postwar period. It also suffered from paint chipping and nose-decal crumbling. Today, a good example is much sought after.

top left: The Evans auto-loader was designed to handle the need for more efficient shipment of automobiles from the factory to the dealer during the 1950s. The Lionel auto-loaders carried four highly detailed model autos on a double rack flatcar. The auto-loaders were all numbered 6414 and were offered with various colors of autos from 1955 to 1966. The green and brown shown here are among the most difficult to find. The multicolored chrome bumper deluxe cars are the easiest to locate. The auto-loader was very popular during its eleven-year production run.

top right: The No. 6416 boat-loader car was made from 1961 to 1963. It used a modified Evans auto-loader body and HO scale boats made by Athearn. The boats seemed much too small for the cabin cruisers they were meant to represent, and sales were not great. Also, during play, the boats and car frequently parted company, making a complete set a desirable item to find today.

above: The No. 6805 atomic waste car was made from 1958 to 1959, during the depths of the Cold War. It was supposed to simulate the transport of spent reactor fuel to a disposal site. The sinister red flashing of the waste containers cast an eerie glow over Lionelville, but the car's very existence was testimony to the almost affectionate—even naive—view Americans had of nuclear power in the 1950s.

The

Postwar

Period

right: Lionel had great success with helicopter cars in the late 1950s and early 1960s. They made ones that fired off a helicopter over Lionelville and ones that simply carried a helicopter as a load. The car pictured is the rare No. 6820 helicopter missile transport car produced from 1960 to 1961. It is unique in that a special missile-carrying section was attached to the helicopter. Today the car is very hard to find complete—that is, with both missiles and the tail cone in place.

below: The No. 6800 flat car with airplane was a popular item and was cataloged from 1957 to 1960. The airplane was a very detailed and pleasing model of a Beechcraft Bonanza, and featured folding wings and landing gear. The plane, which was offered unlettered in various combinations of yellow and black, is difficult to find undamaged, as it was an attractive plaything in its own right. Later in 1962, Lionel reissued the car as No. 6500, with a red and white plane with registration numbers on the wings.

LIONEL LAUNCHES THE
"U-DRIVE" BOAT
ON ITS OWN WATERWAY!
the Backyard Motorboat
that's bathtub safe
floats in 5½" of water
MOTOR DRIVEN

LIONEL — GREAT NEW PLAY VALUE PRODUCTS FOR LAND ... AND SEA!

1964 LIONEL
"O27", "O"
SUPER "O", HO
TRAINS &
ACCESSORIES

above: This prewar crossing gate looks great on a postwar layout, lending to the atmosphere of realism as miniature people scurry by on their way to the trains.

far left: This is a flyer for the U-Drive Boat, another of Lionel's countless attempts to develop a nontrain toy line. The item was unusual, to say the least. It featured a battery-powered boat that a child could ride along a water track, which was designed to be set up in the back yard. The scale of the project is staggering and it is small wonder that only a few were ever sold.

left: The cover of the 1964 catalog was printed in only two colors, reflecting the decline in Lionel train sales. The interior of the catalog was uninspiring and didn't have the lavishness of the catalogs of the 1950s or even the early 1960s.

Lionel presents

Helios 21®

Giant spaceship of the 21st century

Comes with Space Controller...

Anti-Gravity Booster...

in the handsome Helios 21 package.

- **The first lighter-than-air toy ever made that remains buoyant for long periods.**

  Helios 21 is a brand-new concept in toys, made possible by recent discoveries in satellite science.

  This amazing toy defies gravity, because it comes with Lionel's exclusive Anti-Gravity Booster — a completely safe pressurized container which will keep Helios 21 buoyant for months.

- **The first toy ever made that moves in three dimensions by remote control.**

  Helios 21 is propelled up, down, forward, backward, to the right and left by three sturdy electric motors operated from the Space Controller. The Space Controller launches Helios 21 into space, flies it and lands it. Helios 21 will actually hover in space wherever the child guides it. Operates on transformer, power pack or two 6-volt batteries.

- **The first toy made to order for the science-fiction excitement among children from 4 to 12.**

  Going to the moon is already old stuff to the kids. They're ready now for a toy from the 21st century...a giant (43" long) spaceship of the 21st century—Helios 21!

Helios 21 climbs, dives, circles or hovers by remote control. See it demonstrated on television.

a b o v e : Introduced in 1965, the Helios was a Lionel toy that was years ahead of its time. Made of mylar and propelled by miniature motors, the helium-filled blimp could be controlled and made to fly around a room. Similar toys are still made today. The problem was that back then helium was not readily available at party supply stores as it is today. The owner had to buy cannonball-shaped refill tanks that were heavy and difficult to ship. The toy itself worked well and was heavily advertised, but like most of Lionel's other attempts to carve out a nontrain niche, it failed.

r i g h t : In the early 1970s interest in Lionel trains had rebounded to the point where checklists were issued to help collectors keep track of what had been produced. The Ladd checklist is an example of one of these pocket lists. With few or no illustrations they are a far cry from today's elaborate pricing guides.

f a r r i g h t : The Santa Fe F-3 diesel is synonymous with the name Lionel. This master-piece was first introduced in 1948 and was available in one number or another up until 1966. It was the best-selling diesel Lionel ever made, and no wonder. The silver and crimson livery of the Santa Fe Chief even today captures the feel and color of the real train. It evoked dreams of speed and faraway places, and best of all, it ran beautifully. It was the envy of every boy in the 1950s.

COMBINED, ILLUSTRATED

Lionel* Checklist

1929 to 1968

O , 027, 00

&

STANDARD GAUGE

© LADD PUBLICATIONS, INC. 1969

*Lionel is a registered trademark of the Lionel Toy Corp., Hagerstown, Md. 21740

LIONEL

The

Postwar

Period

CHAPTER FOUR

REBIRTH

(1969–2000)

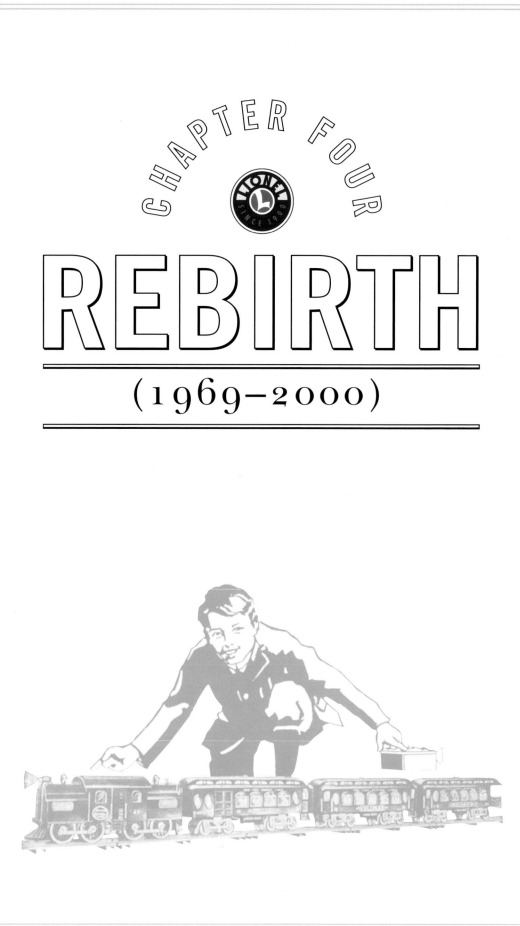

The end of the Lionel trains division in 1969 came as no great surprise. The company had been shifting its main business interests into other areas for years and the train line reflected this slowly changing corporate interest, having degenerated in many cases into cheaply made toys that had none of the old vigor. Also, the competition was gone, now that American Flyer had been bought out by Lionel. The marketing power of HO and N gauge trains, along with the success of slot car racing, had taken a toll on the train market.

And in real life, the United States was increasingly turning away from railroads as a form of transportation.

The company simply did not wish to be in the train business any more because that division was unprofitable, the facilities in New Jersey were costly to maintain, and the last few years had seen much unsold merchandise accumulate. It seemed that O gauge train manufacturing was no longer viable. Lionel began to seek a buyer for the train line and decided to auction off the manufacturing equipment in the Hillside factory.

The tools, dies, plans, and patents, however, were to be offered as a package to interested parties who would keep the train line in production. The name Lionel was still a valuable trademark, after all; in a marketing survey conducted in the early 1970s, Lionel was shown to be a recognized symbol of toy quality.

During this time several cereal companies were expanding into other fields, and one of these fields was toys. The Quaker Oats Company, for example, would eventually absorb Marx Toys. General Mills had aggressively expanded into the toy field in the last few years of the 1960s, for instance, acquiring the Model Products Corporation (MPC) and blending it into its Fundimensions division. Lionel seemed like a natural addition to its brand portfolio.

Negotiations resulted in the arrangement of a lease and royalty plan whereby General Mills put the Lionel train line back into production for 1970 under MPC management. The possibility that Lionel might emerge once again unscathed from apparent doom amazed the toy and hobby world, but General Mills management knew that it would be a formidable task. The train line had been allowed to decline for a number of years, and while Lionel still had the dies and tooling needed for most postwar pieces, they were scattered about and not easily identifiable. Then there were the problems of which items to produce and which level of the market to target for MPC's reentry into the hobby field.

The 1970 poster catalog (it was a large poster on one side and a catalog on the other, folded like a map) featured an ambitious product list, including a double IC diesel, a Great Northern Hudson, and a satellite launching car. Not all of the items were actually made, but the catalog reflected a spirit of optimism that had been missing from Lionel for years and fostered excitement among the train-buying public.

Even though Lionel produced only a basic line of entry-level starter sets and a modest offering of cars, it was clear that the company was

pages 118–119: Shades of Flash Gordon? No, it's Lionel's fantasy loco, the Phantom, issued in 1998. This fun loco is just what its name implies—a fantasy of what might have been if steam locomotives and diesel power had evolved together. Long, sleek, and futuristic, it looks like it would be just as at home sailing through space as along the rails. Art deco at its finest!

above: The return of Lionel in the 1970s prompted an improvement in catalog covers. Bright, colorful, and imaginative, they helped sell Lionel trains during this period of rebirth for the company. The 1973 cover shows the inception of the third generation of Lionel fans.

opposite: The No. 8773 Mickey Mouse loco was issued in 1977 and marked a return of Disney characters to Lionel trains. In time many cars were added to the popular loco, and today some are quite hard to find (and quite valuable as a result).

above: The 1975 and 1976 catalogs marked two highlights in the 1970s for Lionel. Lionel introduced the Spirit of 1776 loco in the 1974 catalog, and added a few cars each year for several years afterward, until there was one for each of the original thirteen states in the Union. And in 1975, Lionel celebrated its seventy-fifth anniversary.

back in the train business again. The marketplace proved to be receptive to new Lionel products, and public response was positive. The old service station and dealer accounts were contacted; it seemed the old Lionel dealer network had survived the lean times. This in itself is amazing because in 1970 the train-collecting hobby was still in its early stages, with few clubs or organizations (by today's standards) promoting the hobby. The positive response to Lionel in 1970 must be attributed to the special place the name Lionel had come to hold in the mind of the American public.

Although all indicators pointed to success, MPC had to reevaluate its market and then revamp its product line accordingly. The marketplace from 1966 to 1970 can be fairly

described as a wasteland for O gauge toy trains. This is not to say that there were not good manufacturers producing specialty items, but until the revitalization of Lionel there was no all-encompassing line that defined the toy train market. The smaller manufacturers had moved in during the decline of Lionel and found a ready market for the items they produced.

Several well-known HO manufacturers attempted to position themselves to take advantage of the economic opportunity. The Atlas Tool Company, a longtime producer of quality HO track, arranged to have a small O scale line produced in Austria and shipped into the United States under the Atlas name. The cars had couplers that would mate with Lionel's—a plus—but the locos, while highly detailed and

modestly priced, were configured for two-rail DC operation. This doomed the line from the start in its efforts to replace Lionel, even though the cars enjoyed brisk sales for a few years until MPC production was in full swing.

Pola of Germany (under the AHM name) also produced a two-rail O gauge line that ran on DC. Their cars, however, did not mate directly with Lionel couplers without modifications. Rivarossi enjoyed limited success, even producing several steam locomotives, until MPC was in full production. A smaller company called Kris Model Trains (KMT), which had purchased the old AMT/KMT (an earlier competitor of Lionel's formed by the merger of American Model Toys and the Kusan Model Trains) tooling, turned out a dizzying array of cattle cars, reefers, boxcars, and gondolas in a huge variety of colors and under a wide range of names. The cars looked good and were compatible with the old Lionel line. KMT enjoyed brisk sales during this time and even produced several illustrated price sheets. However, once MPC entered the scene, the demand for KMT product gradually faded in favor of Lionel.

The reason for MPC's triumph lay in the attitudes of consumers and the company's wise exploitation of the market. It was obvious that the glory days of the 1950s had ended for trains; no longer did American families see a train layout in the house as the social norm. Besides, the lifestyles of Americans had changed, and the conditions that had made the train the toy of choice would never return.

By the early 1970s, two different associations with electric trains had developed in the mind of the public. In the 1950s they had been sold as toys—expensive, high quality toys, but still toys—and the concept of a "collector's item" had not yet arisen. During the 1950s Lionel had occasionally brought back certain items by popular demand, and had implied in some ads that its toys would appreciate in value over time, but the collector angle was not really used to any great extent in marketing. In the 1970s, however, train fans became interested in limited-edition collector's items, something the original Lionel company did not have to deal with and could not have foreseen. MPC also determined that many U.S. consumers still associated trains with Christmas. The company realized that trains around the tree was an American tradition, and that the Christmas market had never really gone away.

Since Christmas sales accounted for only a small part of the year's earnings, MPC decided to divide their marketing efforts in two: Christmas trains and collector trains. Christmas came only once a year, but the collector/nostalgia market promised great opportunities all year long. The baby boomer generation was coming of age and had money to spend. Best of all, they remembered the trains of the 1950s and still seemed fascinated with them. Surely many of them would jump at the chance to buy the unattainable toy of their childhood. Besides, trains had been collected since their first year of production. Lionel, however, was the specialty of only a small group inside the larger world of train hobbyists. The early train collectors of the United States were a small group who usually specialized in Standard Gauge or foreign items. Very few collected the more recent production items, which were viewed as too new and easy to acquire. The baby boomers changed that perception, creating a demand where none had existed before, and trains began to rise in value. Lionel cars and accessories and certain locomotives were now hot items, and train meets and collector's clubs experienced a sudden increase in interest. MPC made plans to offer collector items along with starter sets for beginners and other regular-production train items.

The question was what exactly to produce. For the Christmas market, the starter sets were an easy call, but the collector market was not as easy to predict. In 1970 there were still large numbers of trains available through stores and through private sales. Many items had not yet reached their peak pricing as collectibles since few people sought them out. People had been

---

right: **The No. 140 automatic banjo signal has been a perennial favorite among Lionel enthusiasts ever since it was introduced in 1954. This item has fascinated several generations of train buffs with its wigwag action. The item is still available today, and is still made using the tooling and die work of the original 1954–1966 production run.**

Rebirth

collecting the colorful and attractive 6464 box-car series since it first appeared. Although some were rare, like the B&O Sentinel and the girl's set boxcars, acquiring all of them was not impossible in 1970. In fact, collecting the entire line had become somewhat of a challenge to the collector of Lionel postwar items. A reissue of certain older boxcars might find popularity among those collectors who had not yet found the originals. Also, new names in the line would stimulate further interest in collecting all the boxcars, both the original postwar items and the newly issued MPC models. MPC found itself on the right track when it decided to continue the 6464 type boxcars for these reasons. The

first boxcars were not numbered in the 6464 numbering series, but they continued the spirit of the line and were eagerly snapped up. Even today, boxcars in a multitude of colors and names continue to be a staple Lionel collectible and are always welcomed by collectors.

That settled the question of cars, but what about locos? Again, for the Christmas market there was no question. The cheaper 027 diesels and steamers were resurrected for the starter-set operator market. The collector market pre-sented different concerns. In the early days of Lionel MPC, not all the older tooling and molds had been located, so not every classic piece could be successfully produced. The tooling for

Rebirth

---

left: A view of the Lionel Visitor Center layout engine house shows a variety of locos in residence today; in the center is the No. 18816 C&NW GP-38 (1992). The Visitor Center layout captures the charm of the original Lionel showroom layouts of the 1940s and 1950s.

above: The catalogs of the 1970s reflected an explosion of products and images designed to capture the magic of toy train ownership. For example, the multiracial 1977 catalog cover showed a variety of adults and children playing with Lionel trains, while the 1978 contained shots of the profusion of products Lionel was turning out under MPC ownership.

the GP-7/9 was available, however, and since it was shown in the 1970 poster catalog, the Illinois Central GP-9 was eventually issued, featuring the cheaper 027 motor, no horn, and rubber tires. This may have seemed like a step down from the deluxe Geeps of the 1950s, but it was the first new large diesel since 1966. The model sold well enough to be followed by a dummy two years later, but the shortcomings of the "Pullmor Motor" (a name "borrowed" from American Flyer) soon became apparent, forcing MPC to reconsider. Although many customers were buying trains as shelf pieces, there were still operators out there, and this group was eager to purchase new production items to run with their existing layouts.

In the beginning, many found that the new Lionel products did not live up to the performance standards of the old line (though there was one improvement—the development of needlepoint axles that offered little resistance to the trucks, allowing long trains of heavy cars to glide along with ease). These early criticisms may have had some merit, but one must remember that MPC had not originally envisioned the new Lionel as an exact copy of the original. It took the criticisms to heart anyway, and began a new approach in 1973 with the reintroduction of the famous F-3 diesel. Though these locos featured only one motor (and no sound), it was an updated version of the tried-and-true F-3 motor, and it promised greatly improved performance. In addition, MPC expanded the concept of the "service station" set. The first two sets were merely repackaged regular production items. With the reintroduction of the F-3, the service station sets began to feature unique and limited-issue pieces; they were the first in a long line of collector's sets. The consumer F-3 was to be the B&O, a very hard piece to find from original production. The service station F-3 was the Canadian Pacific, an equally difficult item to obtain from postwar times. Both originals now came at quite a high cost. Lionel offered a

power and a dummy unit for each name, with a single motor based upon the original F-3 motor truck design. A "B" unit was soon issued as a limited-edition item.

The F-3 marked a turning point in the rebirth of Lionel; from now on the emphasis

would be on re-creation of the older, harder-to-find postwar production pieces, items designed to capture the flavor of the golden years. Even at this early date, however, Lionel MPC wasn't interested only in re-creating items from the past, but also improving the operation of these

opposite: The No. 33000 RailScope loco was produced from 1988 to 1990. As it moved along, a small camera in the nose transmitted the image of what was passing by to a small television monitor. Unfortunately, the system consumed nine-volt batteries at an alarming rate (instead of running off the track power) and the picture was in black and white.

above: A Lionel box with a Madison Hardware sticker. Located on Twenty-third Street around the corner from Madison Avenue in New York City, Madison was known for decades as a Lionel mecca that stocked a vast inventory of back stock and obscure parts into the late 1980s, when it was bought out and moved to Detroit by Richard Kughn. The store acquired a legendary status—and its employees a legendary reputation for brusque, unorthodox service—among Lionel collectors, who viewed a trip there as a type of pilgrimage. It was said that if Madison did not have a part, it was not to be found anywhere.

items for the enjoyment of a whole new generation of model train lovers. The sawmill is a good example of this focus. When it was first released in 1956, the sawmill made use of Lionel's vibrator and film loop drive system, in which the flexing of an armature caused by a vibrator coil imparted motion through a string to a drive wheel that could be used to power an accessory. (This system was used also in the cop and hobo car, the aquarium car, and the culvert loaders, among others.) When new, the Vibrotor system worked well enough, but with constant usage it fell out of adjustment. The MPC sawmill copied the No. 464 lumber mill (1956–1960) right down to the original vibrator motor design. When it became apparent that this system had to be improved for the demands of 1980s operation, MPC developed a totally new drive system using a motor; this was more efficient and made the accessory function better than the original in every way. The desire to improve the line's original designs extended to other items as well. Later, the reissued icing station and diesel fueling stations both acquired new motor drives, which improved their operation greatly. Collectors and operators alike appreciated these improvements and bought the reissues in great numbers. MPC's new methods were bearing fruit.

Innovation had long been a characteristic of Lionel, and MPC carried this tradition forward with the introduction in the 1970s of the first working electronic sound system. MPC did not want to reuse the old motor drive whistle, which was costly to produce, or the battery diesel horn system, which had always been problematic in operation. Instead, it created the first circuit board technology for generating sound in its locos. Even the starter sets were given the new "Sound of Steam" chugging system.

Public response was overwhelming. In 1971 Lionel boasted of turning out 3,000 sets a day and of having to expand the facilities 150% to meet the overwhelming demand for trains. Demand was so great that even MPC was caught off guard.

The 1970s were a trying time, what with the end of the Vietnam War, the Watergate scandal, the gas crisis, and the Iranian hostage crisis. It was reassuring that no matter how much things changed or how uncertain the conditions of the world were, Lionel trains, a link to the idealized 1950s, were still being produced. And the public was fascinated with the 1950s. This may have been because the era represented a more innocent period in U.S. history, because it represented the nation at its peak of international prestige, or because it represented the lost youth of the baby boomer generation that was now coming of age. Whatever the cause, love of the 1950s came to be seen in every area of U.S. culture.

The musical *Grease* swept Broadway, *American Graffiti* burst out on movie screens around the country, musical revival groups like Sha Na Na rose in popularity, and *Happy*

Days became a television classic. It was only natural that Lionel trains would catch this wave of nostalgia. Demand for Lionel trains rose and MPC expanded the range of trains it offered. MPC was quick to take advantage of current cultural or social events. To capitalize on the country's bicentennial in 1976, for instance, MPC released a special train set, a loco (the Spirit of '76) and caboose with thirteen cars representing the original thirteen states, over a period of years leading up to the celebration. An instant success, it was followed by several other bicentennial-themed items. Around the same time and following the same marketing approach, MPC offered the Mickey Mouse set, each car of which portrayed a different famous Disney character. This set was purchased by collectors with two different sets of interests: Lionel trains and

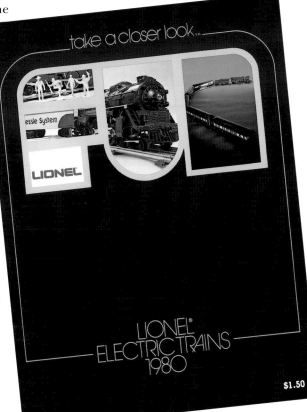

Disney items. Today, both sets are much sought after.

The success of Lionel MPC's reentry into the marketplace had a deep impact on the way trains were sold. In earlier days, consumers who lived in urban areas had bought trains from their local dealer. Those who lived in the country and couldn't make the trek to the city-based dealers were forced to buy by mail, even though there were few companies that offered mail-order services. There was often little difference in cost, as the toy train market did not encourage aggressive competition. By the 1970s, the marketplace had changed dramatically; competition was the norm, and Americans were turning more and more to mail-order companies for their shopping needs. The rebirth of Lionel trains spawned a whole new wave of dealers who were more than willing to cater to the mail-order tastes of the train-buying public. A look at any 1970s model railroad magazine reveals many new firms offering competing prices for Lionel products.

The reintroduction of Lionel trains also led to a growth of train meets across the nation. This unprecedented phenomenon had a great impact on the American model railroad scene. A train meet is best described as a large flea market in which model railroad products and related items are offered for sale. For years, most train meets had been associated with train clubs and were not open to the general public. These early meets were good places for members to socialize and exchange ideas, information, and trains. The train meets that began in the 1970s grew from a different purpose—they were not affiliated with any organization or club and were designed strictly for the purpose of economic exchange. The growth of these independent meets began in the early 1970s. The most notable

above: The 1980 catalog invited the consumer to take a closer look inside at the product. The newly issued O gauge plastic Blue Comet cars are featured prominently in the corner.

area of rapid expansion was the eastern United States, specifically Pennsylvania, New York, and New Jersey. This phenomenon soon spread across the country and came to account for a large share of toy train sales. In addition, new train clubs arose that were devoted to Lionel; these soon became national in scope. Of course, the first train collector organization, the Train Collectors Association (TCA), experienced the greatest growth of any of the meets or organizations during this time period. Americans were buying trains like never before, even more than during the golden age of the 1950s.

To meet the service demands of this expanding market, MPC revitalized and expanded its service station network. This network had stretched across the nation during the 1950s, but it had been allowed to disintegrate as train sales declined in the late 1960s. Under MPC, it became larger than ever. A certain sense of prestige became associated with the service stations, and dealers actively sought to become authorized.

MPC also resumed the publication of service manual sheets to assist with repair. The

Lionel service manual had been like a bible to repairmen of the 1950s. The wealth of information it offered, along with the completeness and clarity of its diagrams, made the original manual indispensable. The new MPC manual grew slowly in completeness and quality until it could claim to be the rightful successor to the original.

In the 1970s the majority of model railway equipment sold nationwide was still HO gauge, despite the impressive gains Lionel had made in O gauge sales in a short time. The quality and variety of HO had improved so dramatically since the 1950s that it was the scale modeler's gauge of choice. Also, the cost and variety of ready-to-run HO sets still offered Lionel O gauge stiff competition for Christmas sales.

In 1974 MPC decided to reenter the HO market with an improved Lionel brand HO electric train. MPC knew that the old Lionel HO line had not been a success, but it believed that modern technology and marketing strategies could make a new line viable. Besides, the size of the HO market was simply too great for a toy company to ignore.

The Lionel MPC engineers soon identified the main problem with the old HO line: the unreliable motor drive system. Using GE motors in the diesels solved this problem, a fact that Lionel was quick to point out in their HO advertising. The second problem was the toy-like appearance of the original HO steam locos. Instead of producing costly new tooling, MPC contracted steam-loco production out to a Pacific Rim manufacturer that had been supplying the American market for years under other brand names. As for cars, they were to be a mix of old Lionel HO and new manufacture.

MPC developed a variety of HO sets, starting with an HO version of the Freedom Train for 1976. New diesel and car designs were also available, along with HO scale buildings. With the release of the Freedom Train and the Daylight loco, MPC HO seemed to be off to a promising start. After the initial burst of

above: This No. 8950 reissue (1979) of the original Virginian TrainMaster diesel locomotive from the postwar era is a beautiful example of Lionel's continued efforts to keep the company's name and legacy of high-quality model trains alive during what was a challenging period in the organization's history. Both the original model and the reissue were based on a Fairbanks-Morse (FM) diesel unit.

opposite: Lionel's 1989 issue of the Amtrak aluminum passenger cars used the same type of design that Lionel pioneered back in the 1950s—extruded aluminum bodies with silhouetted interiors. These passenger cars have been eagerly purchased by modern train operators who want a contemporary railroad name to run on their layouts.

interest, however, sales slackened and consumer interest waned.

The HO line lingered for four years before MPC discontinued it. Poor sales, maintenance problems, and higher costs had all helped to doom it from the start. MPC did not realize that in HO price is the all-important factor, nor did it realize that in the HO realm the brand name Lionel did not have the positive name recognition it had in other toy train formats. Almost every other HO manufacturer could offer a similar product for less, and most had a reputation for quality and durability that Lionel did not have. The reintroduction of HO was a mistake, and it diverted resources away from the main product: O gauge trains.

In another "diversion," around the same time it began experimenting in HO, MPC tried to reach out to the toddler crowd with pull toy trains named Happy Huff n' Puff and Gravel Gus; neither one sold very well, and the toddler train idea was shelved.

Although HO proved to be a failure, MPC had made a wise move with the reintroduction of American Flyer S gauge trains in 1979. (In the early 1970s, a group of investors who had wanted to reintroduce the Flyer line as "Continental Flyer" opened negotiations with MPC. This group even went so far as to advertise the ground-breaking for the Continental Flyer Plant and issue a product list, but in the end no deal was reached and no Continental Flyer was ever made.)

MPC tested the S gauge waters by releasing three cars: a boxcar, a hopper, and a tank car. The response was positive, and MPC was now under pressure to produce a loco. American Flyer locomotives were returned to the scene

opposite: The No. 18006 Reading T-1 is copied directly from the original Reading locomotive. These giants were among the last steam engines built in the United States and several are preserved today. The real T-1's were steel Goliaths, powerhouses on wheels, as anybody who has ridden behind one can attest. Lionel's model, made in 1989, captures all the strength and beauty of these magnificent machines. They grace many Lionel layouts throughout the nation today and are always eagerly sought out at train shows. If you need a real workhorse for your layout, get a Lionel Reading T-1.

below: The long-awaited reissue of the classic Santa Fe marked a milestone for Lionel, with the return of the cab design to the original horn, grab rail, and louver configuration that had been discontinued in the mid-1950s. It is a handsome locomotive and is as stunning as the original one was forty-three years before it.

in the form of a PA-1 freight set and a spectacular Southern Pacific Daylight passenger train. The individual pieces were boxed separately, and both sets were well received by both S collectors and operators, who eagerly demanded more S items.

The success of the reintroduction of S gauge trains stood in sharp contrast to the failure of a new super scale detailed track system earlier in 1973. Made in Italy to Lionel specifications, the new system, called Tru Track, was highly detailed and featured realistic ties and a removable roadbed. It looked great, but no one

had considered the need to make it compatible with the thousands of older locos from the postwar period that were equipped with Magne-Traction. Since MPC had not yet reintroduced Magne-Traction on their locos, little thought had been given to the fact that the new track was made of aluminum, a material upon which Magne-Traction would not work. The system was scrapped and never offered for general sale; the production run was sold off.

To return Lionel to its former glory, MPC conducted an aggressive marketing campaign, developing television commercials for the first

left: Lionel's No. 2037 girl's train, introduced in 1957, was the marketing blunder of the decade. For some inexplicable reason, Lionel marketing people thought girls would like a train set painted in pastel colors and pulled by a pink loco. Nothing was further from the truth— the girls wanted a train that looked like a real one, not an Easter egg on wheels. As a result, the model was a disaster—some dealers even resorted to repainting the trains black in an effort to sell them. Today a complete girl's train with its box is hard to find. Lionel reissued the set in 1991, though that too is hard to find today. It seems yesterday's sales disaster has become today's collector's item. The loco pictured is the 1991 reissue.

above: Lionel always offered a large variety of boxcar names to the public. Lionel found them to be popular items in the 1950s and has continued this realistic line into the modern era. This NYC Pacemaker was modeled after a real car used in the 1950s, and with its gray and red paint scheme is among the most attractive.

time since the 1960s. In November 1976 Lionel sponsored a very successful television special starring Johnny Cash called *Riding the Rails*, which was tied to an ad campaign with Cash as spokesman; this helped boost Lionel sales and bring Lionel back into the national spotlight. The prestige of Lionel was further enhanced later in the 1970s, when the American Association of Railroads made use of Lionel trains in a television ad featuring former astronaut Wally Schirra.

The 1970s were a time of redefining of America's social values, especially with the feminist movement actively promoting equal rights for women. This issue was raised with Lionel when a young girl wrote Lionel a heartfelt letter describing her disappointment with the fact that Lionel was marketing its trains only as boys' toys—no women or girls were included in the ads. The nation became aware of the issue when feminist activists supported the girl's concerns. In response, Lionel moved to include women and girls in the commercials and to promote its trains as toys for all children. The move was generally praised in the press, and Lionel succeeded in extracting itself from a potentially difficult situation.

Some of the highlights of the MPC era were the reintroduction of Lionel's aluminum passenger sets, the TrainMaster FM diesel, and the GG-1 electric locomotive, which caused considerable interest among collectors. Many hopeful train enthusiasts saw these successes as pointing the way to a return of the golden age of the 1950s.

In 1982, General Mills made the disastrous decision to relocate the Lionel manufacturing facilities to Mexico as part of a consolidation move. Unfortunately, the facilities in Mexico were not able to produce items at adequate levels and sales of Lionel products fell dramatically. Also, there was great consumer resistance to Lionel trains not made in the United States (even though they had been made in various parts of the world over the years). In 1985

General Mills admitted its mistake and brought Lionel back to the United States, to Mt. Clemens, Michigan.

In 1984, in a symbolic gesture consciously recalling the glories of the past, Lionel reissued the semi-scale 773 Hudson. Interest in this loco was so great that Lionel used the original 1930s tooling to produce two more issues of it.

In 1985 General Mills began to break up its toy holdings, which were then consolidated under the Fundimensions holding company. Subsequently, Lionel was merged into the Kenner-Parker company. Then, when real estate developer and train collector Richard Kughn learned that Kenner-Parker wanted to unload Lionel, he quickly moved to negotiate a deal. This led to Kughn's establishment of Lionel

opposite: Cabooses are an important part of the Lionel tradition. The company has always sought to offer something special at the tail end of the train, and this Wabash caboose is no exception, with its flashing warning light centered above the door. It flashes an amber light while running or sitting on the track (as long as the track current is on).

above: The No. 12767 steam clean and wheel grind shop accessory is one of the biggest attention-getters among modern Lionel accessories. Introduced in 1992, the grind shop replicates the functions of a modern service area for diesels. When activated, the shop's cleaning rollers revolve and steam jets are emitted as the locomotive passes through while warning bells sound and lights flash. The other function simulates wheels grinding with a shower of real sparks. The engine undergoing service is the GE Dash 9 demonstrator loco (No. 18226), a model commonly seen on U.S. railroads today. Lionel has always taken pains to produce realistic, modern pieces of equipment that were in use on actual railroads throughout the United States going back to the earliest days of the Iron Horse in America.

Trains Inc., and under his leadership a new direction was found for Lionel.

Being a train collector himself, Kughn brought a different perspective to the manufacture and marketing of trains. As a result, Lionel trains entered a new era of realism that to many seemed even better than the classic 1950s.

The most stunning accomplishment came in 1990 with the reissue of the holy grail of trains—the 700E. The factory had to run a four-month assembly schedule to meet the incredible demand for this classic locomotive. Under Kughn's leadership, Lionel struck up a four-year partnership with Samhongsa, Korea's premier train manufacturer, to produce scale items such as the Shay, the T-1, and the S-2 turbine. These engines achieved a new level of realism for Lionel and set the standards for scale excellence in the 1990s. The Lionel Classics—pressed-steel reproductions of selected items from the tinplate period of the 1930s—were also introduced around this time. These reproductions featured the same colors and designs as the original models. Notable examples include the Blue Comet set, the State set, the Auto Race set and the Lionel boats. Lionel Classics attracted considerable interest among collectors and are actively sought after in today's marketplace. The Kughn era created a rich legacy of quality and quantity. Many feel that he was responsible

above: Tank cars have always been fascinating to model railroaders because of the variety of names and colors they feature. This is a Johnson Company chemical car (1991). Note the end markings on the tank and the reporting marks on the side. It is these little details that have always made Lionel products stand out.

opposite: The smoking roadside diner is a wonderful accessory that captures the bygone days of U.S. railroading, when every rail yard had a twenty-four-hour eatery nearby that was frequented by the railway workers. This model features illuminated silhouette windows, parking lot lights, and a smoking exhaust stack. It looks so real you can almost smell the hamburgers frying on the grill.

for the rapid growth of the O gauge hobby during the 1980s and into the 1990s.

Innovations in electronic technology were also encouraged during the Kughn years. One of the most ingenious inventions was the RailScope TV system. This system allowed the transmission of a black and white TV picture of the track from the cab of the locomotive as it raced along the layout. The system worked well enough, but because it required a large number of batteries and wore them out after only about thirty minutes, the public did not overwhelmingly accept it. Attempts to extend the battery life with a backup pack or railpower pickup did not boost RailScope's sales. The system was offered in the catalog in several gauges, but only HO, G, and O RailScope locos were actually produced. The system was discontinued

above: The No. 12936 intermodal crane is an exciting new accessory made by Lionel in the 1990s and faithfully duplicates all the action found in a modern intermodal container yard. This Southern Pacific issue was produced in 1997 and can be found on many layouts today.

right: The Western Maryland Shay was one of most attention-getting locomotives Lionel ever made. These geared locos were designed for industrial and branch line use in specific industries like logging. This model is superb, with all the working gearing and drive rods of the original engine; the motion of the intricate drive is truly a treat to watch. The detailing of this model set a new standard for Lionel and paved the way for the greater scale realism of the Lionel trains of today.

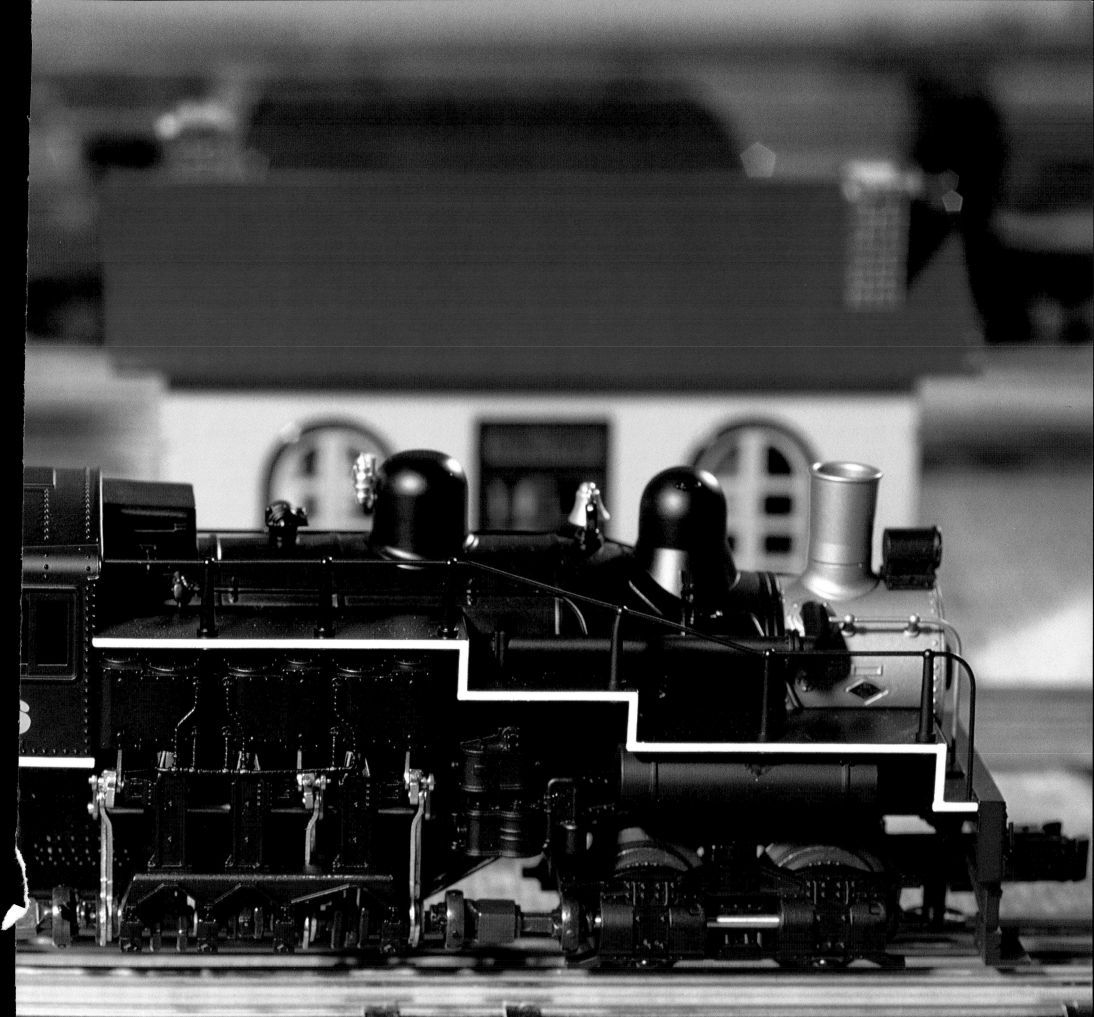

after only a few years, and it disappeared from the catalog.

However, one innovation from the era did prove to be important: the RailSounds locomotive systems, which used digital chip technology to recreate the sounds of actual locomotives.

Desiring to further this aspect of Lionel's product development, rock legend Neil Young, who had experimented on his own with model train control and sound systems, formed a partnership with Kughn in 1992 called Liontech to provide Lionel with exclusive state-of-the-art sound and control systems. The first product of the Liontech partnership was RailSounds II, which featured sounds recorded from real locomotives. This new sound system positioned Lionel as a leader in model railroad technology.

The big breakthrough for Lionel and Liontech came in 1994: the unveiling of the TrainMaster control system for model trains, which allowed for complete and independent control of any AC-powered locomotive on a layout. In many ways, this system was the fulfillment of the unrealized potential of the postwar electronic set.

In 1995 Kughn decided to sell Lionel. He eventually made a deal with Wellspring Associates, an investment firm that included Neil Young among its investors. In 1996 Wellspring issued the first fully illustrated Lionel catalog since the postwar period. In 1996, with the company centenary only four years away, Wellspring created a special Lionel Century Club, whose members would be offered unique Lionel pieces. The new management also brought back many classic products from the 1950s, all equipped with the TrainMaster system. At the same time, Wellspring also decided to produce a variety of other items to accommodate a variety of tastes, including new cartoon-themed cars like Rocky and Bullwinkle, current-interest items like "alien transport" cars, and holiday-themed cars for Halloween, Valentine's Day, and Easter. Wellspring also announced the most spectacular offering yet: Lionel's first articulated locomotive, a giant Allegheny, a fitting close to a century of train making and a stunning kickoff for the next century of Lionel.

There's never been a better time to own Lionel trains and to enjoy this company's rich heritage, whether you are interested in collecting, operating, or just playing with trains with your family. So buy a train, get on board, and see what makes Lionel such a beloved and enduring icon.

above: The reissued fireman car captures all the features of the late-1950s original, including a flashing light, a moveable ladder, and a rotating fireman. While not exactly a prototypical car, it was loads of fun to play with then, and still is now.

Lionel tried out space-age cars in the years after the Sputnik launch in 1957. They were originally greeted with mixed consumer response, but today they are sought-after collectors items. Lionel has slowly rereleased many of them. The missile launching car (No. 16718, right) and radar car (No. 16652, below) are two of the most famous such reissues. The missile car raises up an IRBM (intermediate range ballistic missile) on its launching beam and fires the missile when the ramp reaches the top of its cycle. The radar car scans the track for enemy activity with a rotating radar screen while the operator monitors all on his display. Realistic? Maybe not. Exciting? You bet.

right: Lionel freight cars have always been faithful copies of the items used on real railroads. Here we see a Lionel refrigerator car and a newer waffle-side boxcar. The bodies of the cars copy all the detail of the originals, down to the wood siding.

below: This is the B unit from the No. 18120 modern reissue of the No. 2023 fiftieth anniversary loco shown on page 75. It features the exact colors of the original as well as its die-cast frame. It is a testament to Lionel's concern for creating reissues as close to the original form and color as possible.

opposite: This looks like an old prewar loco, right? Wrong! This is the 1996 successor to Lionel's 700E. It is the No. 18045 Commodore Vanderbilt, designed in real life by the New York Central in the 1930s and named after the railroad's founder. The loco is a scale model with full detail and is a reminder that Lionel can still build them like they used to. Note the streamlined boiler, which is in keeping with notions about speed in the 1930s, when everything from toasters to locos were given a sleek, aerodynamic look. This art deco styling belies the model's recent vintage.

opposite: The No. 262 highway light and gate was originally issued in the 1960s and was carried over into modern times. The gate lowers and lights come on when a train passes the crossing it protects. The gate has always been a popular accessory, and is found on most home layouts. It is usually among the first accessories purchased by new Lionel owners.

above: A railway worker peers out of the open door of a Western Pacific "Shock Protected Freight" box car on a siding where it has been spotted by the switcher for unloading. With their sliding doors and attention to detail, Lionel box cars enhance detailed scenes such as this one, which add touches of realism to the model railway.

above: This modern Lionel locomotive (No. 18654) captures all the rugged realism of the 1950s model it copies. As it rests next to a Lionel station between assignments on a model railroad, the loco's massive die-cast boiler and plated side rods reflect a bygone era in U.S. railroading.

opposite: The Lionel Southern Pacific GS-2 and GS-4 locos were conceived during the 1950s but never made. Lionel issued several different versions in the 1980s and 1990s. The loco is a perennial favorite with its Daylight black, orange, and red paint scheme. Because of the loco's art deco styling, many Lionel operators favor the Southern Pacific for their modern layouts, along with a matching set of passenger cars. This issue, No. 18071, a model of loco No. 4449, was made in 1998 and features the TrainMaster control system.

right: "Stunning" is the best word to describe the huge **C&O Allegheny (No. 28011)**, a masterpiece of engineering skill and one of the biggest locomotives Lionel has produced to date. The giant loco features a complete sound system, smoke, highly detailed die-cast metal construction, and museum-like precision in detailing. Lionel also released the spectacular 4-8-8-4 Union Pacific Big Boy (No. 28029) at the end of 1999. The Allegheny and Big Boy point the way to the new millennium for Lionel and the model railroad hobby. If these locomotives are any indication of what is to come in the next century, it will surely be the best of times for toy train enthusiasts.

Ambrose, Paul V. *Greenberg's Guide to Lionel Trains 1945–1969: Cataloged Sets*, vol. 3. Waukesha, Wisconsin: Kalmbach Books, 1999

_____. *Greenberg's Guide to Lionel Trains 1945–1969: Motive Power and Rolling Stock*, vol. 1. Waukesha, Wisconsin: Greenberg Books, 1996.

_____. *Greenberg's Guide to Lionel Trains 1945–1969: Rare and Unusual*, vol. 5. Waukesha, Wisconsin: Greenberg Books, 1993.

Ambrose, Paul V., and Harold J. Lovelock. *Greenberg's Guide to Lionel Trains 1945–1969: Selected Variations*, vol. 7. Waukesha, Wisconsin: Greenberg Books, 1993.

Algozzini, Joseph P., and Paul V. Ambrose. *Greenberg's Guide to Lionel Trains 1945–1969: Uncatalogued Sets*, vol. 4. Sykesville, Maryland: Greenberg Publishing Company, 1992.

Fraely, Donald, ed. *Lionel Trains: Standard of the World 1900–1943*, 2nd ed. Strasburg, Pennsylvania: Train Collector's Association, 1989.

Grams, John. *Beginner's Guide to Toy Train Collecting and Operating*. Waukesha, Wisconsin: Kalmbach Books, 1991.

Greenberg, Bruce C. *Greenberg's Guide to Lionel Trains 1901–1942: Standard Gauge*, vol. 1. Sykesville, Maryland: Greenberg Publishing Company, 1994.

Hollander, Ron. *All Aboard! The Story of Joshua Lionel Cowen and His Lionel Train Company*. New York, New York: Workman Publishing, 1981.

LaVoie, Roland E. *Greenberg's Guide to Lionel Trains 1970–1991: Motive Power and Rolling Stock*, vol. 1. Waukesha, Wisconsin: Greenberg Books, 1991.

_____. *Greenberg's Guide to Lionel Trains 1970–1997: Accessories*, vol. 3. Waukesha, Wisconsin: Kalmbach Books, 1997.

McComas, Tom, Charles Krone, and Todd Wagner. *Lionel Price and Rarity Guide 1970–1999*, vol. 2. New Buffalo, Michigan: TM Books and Video Inc., 1998.

McComas, Tom, and James Tuohy. *Lionel Collector's Guide and History: Prewar O Gauge*, vol. 1. Radnor, Pennsylvania: Chilton Book Company, 1975.

_____. *Lionel Collector's Guide and History: Postwar*, vol. 2. Radnor, Pennsylvania: Chilton Book Company, 1976.

_____. *Lionel Collector's Guide and History: Standard Gauge*, vol. 3. Radnor, Pennsylvania: Chilton Book Company, 1978.

_____. *Lionel Collector's Guide and History: 1970–1980*, vol. 4. Radnor, Pennsylvania: Chilton Book Company, 1980.

_____. *Lionel Collector's Guide and History: The Archives*, vol. 5. Radnor, Pennsylvania: Chilton Book Company, 1981.

_____. *Lionel Collector's Guide and History: Advertising and Art*, vol. 6. Radnor, Pennsylvania: Chilton Book Company, 1981.

McEntarfer, David. *Greenberg's Guide to Lionel Trains 1901–1942: Prewar Sets*, vol. 4. Waukesha, Wisconsin: Greenberg Books, 1995.

Osterhoff, Robert. *Greenberg's Guide to Lionel Paper and Collectibles*. Sykesville, Maryland: Greenberg Publishing Company, 1990.

Riddle, Peter H. *Greenberg's Guide to Lionel Trains 1901–1942: Accessories*, vol. 3. Sykesville, Maryland: Greenberg Publishing Company, 1993.

Stewart, Alan. *Greenberg's Guide to Lionel Trains 1945–1969: Accessories*, vol. 6. Waukesha, Wisconsin: Greenberg Books, 1994.

Various. *On the Right Track: The History of Lionel Trains: 1900–1975*. Fundimensions Division of General Mills Fun Group Inc., 1975.

opposite: **What better way to end our history of Lionel trains than with a friendly wave from a toy conductor on the platform of a Lionel tinplate caboose (No. 217). Lionel is on track and has a green light to steam though another 100 years of model railroading fun!**

ONLINE SOURCES

www.lionel.com

The official Lionel company website is a great source of information on all facets of Lionel model railroading. There's a Dealer Locator feature, Hints for Hobbyists, Lionel History, A Gift Shop, Notes for Parents, Guidelines for Collectors, Listings of Shows & Events, Downloadable Sound and Graphic Files, Links to Related Sites, and much more.

LIONEL SPONSORED CLUBS

Lionel Railroader Club

Climb aboard the Lionel Railroader Club and get on the "Inside Track"! As an LRRC member, you'll read the latest insider scoops in our newsletter, receive Lionel catalogs hot off the presses and be eligible for members-only purchases and discounts. Information can be found at www.lionel.com under their "Clubs" section.

Ambassador Club

The Lionel Ambassador Program is a volunteer organization of Lionel Railroading enthusiasts who want to share the joy of the hobby with others. The Ambassador Program requires no financial commitment, and it's not a distinction earned by the number of Lionel purchases made.

Ambassador status is an honor granted in recognition of your knowledge of and enthusiasm for Lionel model railroading—particularly our proud tradition of bringing family and friends together in the spirit of fun and fellowship.

MAGAZINES

Classic Toy Trains magazine

Fascinated by toy trains of the past and present? We are, too. *Classic Toy Trains* magazine is a superb source of information for lovers of Lionel, American Flyer, MTH, Marx, K–Line, Ives, and other toy trains dating from 1900 to today.
http://www.kalmbach.com/ctt/toytrains.html
Subscriptions: 800-533-6644

O Gauge Railroading magazine

Each Issue Brings You: Spectacular Layouts • New Product Reviews • Repair Tips from Jim Barrett • Collector's Gallery • Do-It-Yourself Projects • Industry News • Current Hobby News • Listings of Events, Shows and Conventions
http://members.aol.com/OGaugeRwy/ogr.html
Subscriptions: 610-759-0406

INDEPENDENT CLUBS

Lionel Operating Trains Society (LOTS)
6367 West Fork Rd
Cincinnati, Ohio 45247

A non-profit club with more than 2,500 members throughout the world, LOTS was founded in 1979, and is dedicated to promoting the enjoyment of operating of Lionel and compatible trains and accessories. In their own words: Our small but friendly band of model train enthusiasts is dedicated to having the most fun possible operating and collecting those wonderful trains from yesteryear and today—Lionel! Yes, those fascinating milk cars, searchlight cars, and Santa Fe diesels that you remember from the 1940s and 1950s are still out there, lovingly cared for by a new generation of hobbyists, as are the new versions being made by modern Lionel! The members of LOTS come from all walks of life, united by their love of these trains and all the skills and enjoyment which result from setting up and running them on model layouts. Many have different interests: scenery, electronics, operations, lighting, accessories, repairing motors, or even operating some of the fine related products from other O-gauge manufacturers such as K-Line, Weaver, Williams, or Mike's Train House. The common denominator is fun!
http://www.lots-trains.org

Toy Train Operating Society (TTOS)
25 W. Walnut Street
Suite 308
Pasadena, CA 91103

Membership in the Toy Train Operating Society leads to much fun because it supports collecting and operating both new and old trains and preserves the historical impact of this popular American tradition. TTOS, a non-profit organization founded in 1966, is international in scope with twenty-three active divisions. Yearly membership, for a modest fee, includes six issues of the TTOS Bulletin, six issues of the TTOS Order Board, a National Membership Directory, and eligibility for National Conventions and limited edition convention cars and other special offers.
Membership: 626-578-0673
http://www.ttos.org

The Train Collectors Association (TCA)
National Business Office
P.O. Box 248
Strasburg, PA. 17579

Headquartered in Strasburg, Pennsylvania, the TCA is one of the largest and most prestigious collecting societies in the world. Our Mission: To preserve an important segment of history—Tinplate Toy Trains—through research, education, community outreach, and fellowship, and to promote the growth and enjoyment of the hobby. Membership in the Association has grown from a humble beginning of sixty-eight meeting in a barn in Pennsylvania to a worldwide organization of over 31,000 members in twenty Divisions with twenty Chapters.
http://www.traincollectors.org

INDEX